# Car Dealership Accounting

Steven M. Bragg

**AccountingTools®**

ISBN-13: 978-1-64221-149-8

For more information about AccountingTools® products, visit our Web site at www.accountingtools.com.

# Table of Contents

# About the Author

**Steven Bragg, CPA,** has been the chief financial officer or controller of four companies, as well as a consulting manager at Ernst & Young. He received a master's degree in finance from Bentley College, an MBA from Babson College, and a Bachelor's degree in Economics from the University of Maine. He has been a two-time president of the Colorado Mountain Club, and is an avid alpine skier, mountain biker, and certified master diver. Mr. Bragg resides in Centennial, Colorado. He has written more than 300 books and courses, including *New Controller Guidebook*, *GAAP Guidebook*, and *Payroll Management*.

Steven maintains the accountingtools.com web site, which contains continuing professional education courses, the Accounting Best Practices podcast, and thousands of articles on accounting subjects.

---

# Car Dealership Accounting

## Introduction

There is a great deal of complexity involved in running the accounting system for a car dealership, because of the many profit centers within the organization. In order to ascertain whether these profit centers are generating a profit, the accountant must be able to correctly assign revenues and expenses to the profit centers, while also tracking substantial amounts of vehicle and parts inventory, and processing payroll for large numbers of employees. In the following pages, we cover the essential elements of this challenging accounting environment.

## Recording Transactions in an Accounting System

A *transaction* is a business event that has a monetary impact on a dealership's financial statements, and is recorded as an entry in its accounting records. Examples of transactions are paying a supplier for goods delivered, paying an employee for hours worked, and receiving payment from a customer.

How do you record a transaction in your accounting system? In most cases, the software manufacturer has developed a simple form structure, so you simply click on the transaction type (such as a customer billing or a cash receipt) and then fill in the form that has been presented to you. In other cases, a more specialized format is called for, which is a journal entry. Before we delve into journal entries, you will need to understand the concept of double entry accounting.

### Double Entry Accounting

*Double entry accounting* is a record keeping system under which every transaction is recorded in at least two accounts. There is no upper limit on the number of accounts used in a transaction, but the minimum is two accounts. There are two columns in each account, with debit entries on the left and credit entries on the right. In double entry accounting, the total of all debit entries must match the total of all credit entries. When this happens, a transaction is said to be *in balance*. If the totals do not agree, the transaction is *out of balance*. An out of balance transaction must be corrected before financial statements can be created.

The definitions of a debit and credit are:

- A *debit* is an accounting entry that either increases an asset or expense account, or decreases a liability or equity account. It is positioned to the left in an accounting entry.
- A *credit* is an accounting entry that either increases a liability or equity account, or decreases an asset or expense account. It is positioned to the right in an accounting entry.

An account is a separate, detailed record associated with a specific asset, liability, equity, revenue, expense, gain, or loss. Examples of accounts are noted in the following table.

**Characteristics of Sample Accounts**

| Account Name | Account Type | Normal Account Balance |
| --- | --- | --- |
| Cash | Asset | Debit |
| Accounts receivable | Asset | Debit |
| Vehicle inventory | Asset | Debit |
| Fixed assets | Asset | Debit |
| Accounts payable | Liability | Credit |
| Loans payable | Liability | Credit |
| Common stock | Equity | Credit |
| Retained earnings | Equity | Credit |
| Revenue | Revenue | Credit |
| Cost of sales | Expense | Debit |
| Compensation expense | Expense | Debit |
| Utilities expense | Expense | Debit |
| Travel and entertainment | Expense | Debit |
| Gain on sale of asset | Gain | Credit |
| Loss on sale of asset | Loss | Debit |

The key point with double entry accounting is that a single transaction always triggers a recordation in *at least* two accounts, as assets and liabilities gradually flow through a dealership and are converted into revenues, expenses, gains, and losses.

## The Accruals Concept

An *accrual* is a journal entry that is used to recognize revenues and expenses that have been earned or consumed, respectively, and for which the related source documents have not yet been received or generated. Accruals are needed to ensure that all revenue and expense elements are recognized within the correct reporting period, irrespective of the timing of related cash flows. Without accruals, the amount of revenue, expense, and profit or loss in a period will not necessarily reflect the actual level of economic activity within a business. Accruals are a key part of the closing process used to create financial statements under the accrual basis of accounting; without accruals, financial statements would be considerably less accurate.

It is most efficient to initially record most accruals as reversing entries. This is a useful feature when a dealership is expecting to issue an invoice to a customer or receive an invoice from a supplier in the following period. For example, an accountant may know that a supplier invoice for $20,000 will arrive a few days after the end of a month, but she wants to close the books as soon as possible. Accordingly, she records a $20,000 reversing entry to recognize the expense in the current month. In the next month, the accrual reverses, creating a negative $20,000 expense that is offset by the arrival and recordation of the supplier invoice.

Examples of accruals that a business might record are:

- *Expense accrual for interest.* A local lender issues a loan to a dealership, and sends the borrower an invoice each month, detailing the amount of interest owed. The dealership can record the interest expense in advance of invoice receipt by recording accrued interest.
- *Expense accrual for wages.* A dealership pays its employees once a month for the hours they have worked through the 26th day of the month. The firm can accrue all additional wages earned from the 27th through the last day of the month, to ensure that the full amount of the wage expense is recognized.

If a dealership records its transactions under the cash basis of accounting, it does not use accruals. Instead, the organization records transactions only when it either pays out or receives cash.

## Journal Entries

Journal entries are used in a double entry accounting system, where the intent is to record every business transaction in at least two places. For example, when a dealership sells products for cash, this increases both the revenue account and the cash account. Or, if supplies inventory is acquired on account, this increases both the accounts payable account and the inventory account.

The structure of a journal entry is:

- A header line may include a journal entry number and entry date.
- The first column includes the account number and account name into which the entry is recorded. This field is indented if it is for the account being credited.
- The second column contains the debit amount to be entered.
- The third column contains the credit amount to be entered.
- A footer line may also include a brief description of the reason for the entry.

Thus, the basic journal entry format is:

|  | Debit | Credit |
|---|---|---|
| Account name / number | $xx,xxx |  |
|     Account name / number |  | $xx,xxx |

The structural rules of a journal entry are that there must be a minimum of two line items in the entry, and that the total amount entered in the debit column equals the total amount entered in the credit column.

A journal entry is usually printed and stored in a binder of accounting transactions, with backup materials attached that justify the entry.

There are several types of journal entries, including the following:

- *Adjusting entry.* An adjusting entry is used at month-end to alter the financial statements to bring them into compliance with the relevant accounting rules and regulations. For example, a dealership could accrue unpaid wages at month-end in order to recognize the wages expense in the current period.
- *Compound entry.* This is a journal entry that includes more than two lines of entries. It is frequently used to record complex transactions, or several transactions at once. For example, the journal entry to record a payroll usually contains many lines, since it involves the recordation of numerous tax liabilities and payroll deductions.
- *Reversing entry.* This is an adjusting entry that is reversed as of the beginning of the following period, usually because an expense was accrued in the preceding period, and is no longer needed. Thus, a wage accrual in the preceding period is reversed in the next period, to be replaced by an actual payroll expenditure.

In general, journal entries are not used to record high-volume transactions, such as customer billings or supplier invoices. These transactions are handled through specialized software modules that present a standard online form to be filled out. Once the form is complete, the software automatically creates the accounting record.

The following journal entry examples are intended to provide an outline of the general structure of the more common entries encountered. It is impossible to provide a complete set of journal entries that address every variation on every situation, since there are thousands of possible entries.

In each of the following journal entries, we state the topic, the relevant debit and credit, and additional comments as needed.

Revenue journal entries:

- *Sales entry.* Debit accounts receivable and credit revenue. If a sale is for cash, the debit is to the cash account instead of the accounts receivable account.
- *Allowance for doubtful accounts entry.* Debit bad debt expense and credit the allowance for doubtful accounts. When actual bad debts are identified, debit the allowance account and credit the accounts receivable account, thereby clearing out the associated invoice.

Expense journal entries:

- *Accounts payable entry*. Debit the asset or expense account to which a purchase relates and credit the accounts payable account. When an account payable is paid, debit accounts payable and credit the cash account.
- *Payroll entry*. Debit the wages expense and payroll tax expense accounts, and credit the cash account. There may be additional credits to account for deductions from benefit expense accounts, if employees have permitted deductions for benefits to be taken from their pay.
- *Accrued expense entry*. Debit the applicable expense and credit the accrued expenses liability account. This entry is usually reversed automatically in the following period.
- *Depreciation entry*. Debit depreciation expense and credit accumulated depreciation. These accounts may be categorized by type of fixed asset.

Asset journal entries:

- *Cash reconciliation entry*. This entry can take many forms, but there is usually a debit to the bank fees account to recognize changes made by the bank, with a credit to the cash account. There may also be a debit to office supplies expense for any check supplies purchased and paid for through the bank account.
- *Prepaid expense adjustment entry*. When recognizing prepaid expenses as expenses, debit the applicable expense account and credit the prepaid expense asset account.
- *Fixed asset addition entry*. Debit the applicable fixed asset account and credit accounts payable.
- *Fixed asset derecognition entry*. Debit accumulated depreciation and credit the applicable fixed asset account. There may also be a gain or loss on the asset derecognition.

Liability journal entries:

See the preceding accounts payable and accrued expense entries.

Equity journal entries:

- *Dividend declaration*. Debit the retained earnings account and credit the dividends payable account. Once dividends are paid, this is a debit to the dividends payable account and a credit to the cash account.
- *Stock sale*. Debit the cash account and credit the common stock account.

These journal entry examples are only intended to provide an overview of the general types and formats of accounting entries. There are many variations on the entries presented here that are used to deal with a broad range of business transactions.

## The Ledger Concept

Accounting information is stored in a computerized ledger. A *ledger* is a database in which double-entry accounting transactions are stored or summarized. A *subsidiary ledger* is a ledger designed for the storage of specific types of accounting transactions. If a subsidiary ledger is used, the information in it is then summarized and posted to an account in the *general ledger*, which in turn is used to construct the financial statements of a dealership. The account in the general ledger where this summarized information is stored is called a *control account*. Most accounts in the general ledger are not control accounts; instead, transactions are recorded directly into them.

A subsidiary ledger can be set up to offload data storage for virtually any general ledger account. However, they are usually only created for areas in which there are high transaction volumes, which limits their use to a few areas. Examples of subsidiary ledgers are:

- Accounts receivable ledger
- Fixed assets ledger
- Inventory ledger
- Purchases ledger

> **Tip:** Subsidiary ledgers are used when there is a large amount of transaction information that would clutter up the general ledger. This situation typically arises in companies with significant sales volume. Thus, there may be no need for subsidiary ledgers in a smaller dealership.

As an example of the information in a subsidiary ledger, the inventory ledger may contain transactions pertaining to receipts into stock, movements of parts to the parts counter, and sales of parts to customers.

In order to research accounting information when a subsidiary ledger is used, drill down from the general ledger to the appropriate subsidiary ledger, where the detailed information is stored. Consequently, if there is a preference to conduct as much research as possible within the general ledger, use fewer subsidiary ledgers.

The following chart shows how the various data entry modules within an accounting system are used to create transactions which are recorded in either the general ledger or various subsidiary ledgers, and which are eventually aggregated to create the financial statements.

## Transaction Flow in the Accounting System

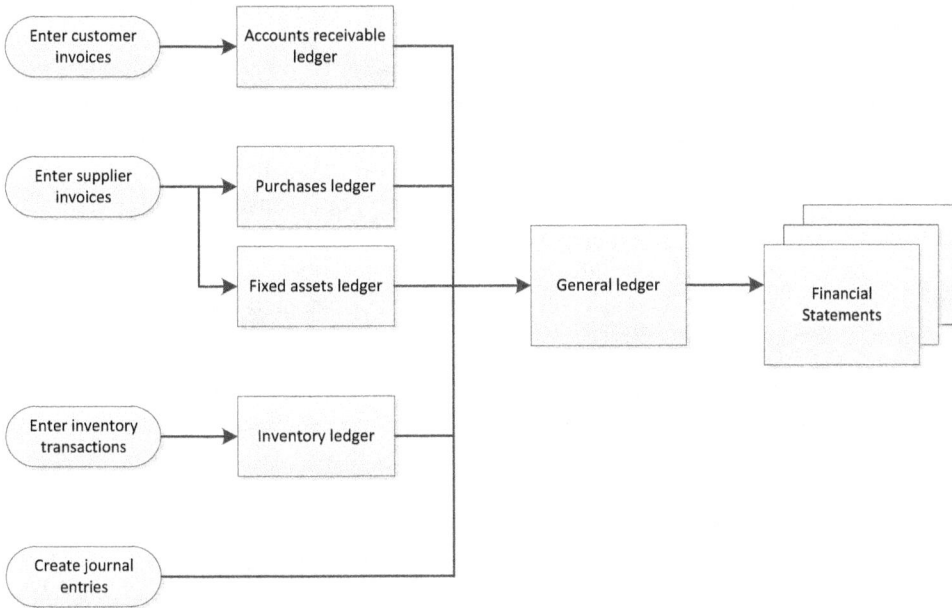

```
Enter customer          Accounts receivable
invoices        ───►    ledger

Enter supplier
invoices        ───►    Purchases ledger

                        Fixed assets ledger  ───►  General ledger  ───►  Financial
                                                                          Statements

Enter inventory
transactions    ───►    Inventory ledger

Create journal
entries
```

## Posting to the General Ledger

*Posting* refers to the aggregation of financial transactions from where they are stored in subsidiary ledgers, and transferring this information into the general ledger. Information in one of the subsidiary ledgers is aggregated at regular intervals, at which point a summary-level entry is made and posted in the general ledger. In a manual bookkeeping environment, the aggregation may occur at fixed intervals, such as once a day or once a month. For example, if the source ledger were the accounts receivables ledger, the aggregated posting entry might include a debit to the accounts receivable account, and credits to the sales account and various sales tax liability accounts. When posting this entry in the general ledger, a notation could be made in the description field, stating the date range to which the entry applies.

In a computerized bookkeeping environment, posting to the general ledger may be unnoticeable. The software simply does so at regular intervals, or asks if you want to post, and then handles the underlying general ledger posting automatically. It is possible that no posting transaction even appears in the reports generated by the system.

Posting to the general ledger does not occur for lower-volume transactions, which are already recorded in the general ledger. For example, fixed asset purchases may be so infrequent that there is no need for a subsidiary ledger to house these transactions, so they are instead recorded directly in the general ledger.

**General Ledger Overview**

A general ledger is the master set of accounts in which is summarized all transactions occurring within a dealership during a specific period of time. The general ledger contains all of the accounts currently being used, and is sorted by account number. Either individual transactions or summary-level postings from subsidiary ledgers are listed within each account number, and are sorted by transaction date. Each entry in the general ledger includes a reference number that states the source of the information. The source may be a subsidiary ledger, a journal entry, or a transaction entered directly into the general ledger.

The format of the general ledger varies somewhat, depending on the accounting software being used, but the basic set of information presented for an account within the general ledger is:

- *Transaction number.* The software assigns a unique number to each transaction, so that it can be more easily located in the accounting database if the transaction number is known.
- *Transaction date.* This is the date on which the transaction was entered into the accounting database.
- *Description.* This is a brief description that summarizes the reason for the entry.
- *Source.* Information may be forwarded to the general ledger from a variety of sources, so the report should state the source, in case there is a need to go back to the source to research the reason for the entry.
- *Debit and credit.* States the amount debited or credited to the account for a specific transaction.

The following sample of a general ledger report shows a possible format that could be used to present information for several transactions that are aggregated under a specific account number.

## Sample General Ledger Presentation

| Trans. No. | Trans. Date | Description | Source | Debit | Credit |
|---|---|---|---|---|---|
| **Acct. 10400** | | **Acct: Accounts Receivable** | | **Beginning balance** | **$127,500.00** |
| 10473 | 3/22/xx | Customer invoice | ARL | 93.99 | |
| 10474 | 3/23/xx | Customer invoice | ARL | 47.80 | |
| 10475 | 3/24/xx | Credit memo | ARL | | 43.17 |
| 10476 | 3/25/xx | Customer invoice | ARL | 65.25 | |
| 18903 | 3/26/xx | Cash receipt | CRJ | | 1,105.20 |
| | | | | **Ending balance** | **$126,558.67** |

It is extremely easy to locate information pertinent to an accounting inquiry in the general ledger, which makes it the primary source of accounting information. For example:

- A manager reviews the balance sheet and notices that the amount of debt appears too high. The accountant looks up the debt account in the general ledger and sees that a loan was added at the end of the month.
- A manager reviews the income statement and sees that the bad debt expense for his profit center is very high. The accountant looks up the expense in the general ledger, drills down to the source journal entry, and sees that a new bad debt projection was the cause of the increase in bad debt expense.

As the examples show, the source of an inquiry is frequently the financial statements; when conducting an investigation, the accountant begins with the general ledger, and may drill down to source documents from there to ascertain the reason(s) for an issue.

## Cash Basis vs. Accrual Basis Accounting

The *accrual basis of accounting* is the concept of recording revenues when earned and expenses as incurred. This concept differs from the *cash basis of accounting*, under which revenues are recorded when cash is received, and expenses are recorded when cash is paid. For example, a dealership operating under the accrual basis of accounting will record a sale as soon as it issues an invoice to a customer, while a cash basis business would instead wait to be paid before it records the sale. Similarly, an accrual basis organization will record an expense as incurred, while a cash basis business would instead wait to pay its supplier before recording the expense.

The accrual basis tends to provide more even recognition of revenues and expenses over time than the cash basis, and so is considered the most valid accounting system for ascertaining the results of operations and financial position of a business. In particular, it supports the *matching principle*, under which revenues and all related expenses are to be recorded within the same reporting period; by doing so, it should be possible to see the full extent of the profits and losses associated with specific business transactions within a single reporting period.

---

**EXAMPLE**

Smith Automotive repairs a customer's car in February, for which it invoices the customer $5,000, to be paid in 30 days. The dealership also incurs $200 of parts costs on its debit card, for which payment is immediately extracted from the firm's bank account. Under the accrual basis of accounting, both the revenue and expense would appear in the February income statement, showing the full impact of the job. However, under the cash basis of accounting, only the parts cost would appear as an expense in February, with the customer billing appearing a month or two later, when the customer pays the bill.

---

The accrual basis requires the use of estimated reserves in certain areas. For example, a dealership should recognize an expense for estimated bad debts that have not yet been incurred. By doing so, all expenses related to a revenue transaction are recorded at the same time as the revenue, which results in an income statement that fully reflects the results of operations. These estimates may not be entirely accurate, and so can lead to materially inaccurate financial statements. Consequently, care must be used when estimating reserves.

The cash basis of accounting requires little accounting knowledge to operate. Nonetheless, this approach to recording transactions suffers from the following problems:

- *Accuracy*. The cash basis yields less accurate results than the accrual basis of accounting, since the timing of cash flows does not necessarily reflect the proper timing of changes in the financial condition of a business. Generally, cash basis accounting tends to result in more reported peaks and valleys in financial performance, due to the lumpy nature of revenue and (especially) expense recognition.
- *Manipulation*. A dealership can alter its reported results by not cashing received checks or altering the payment timing for its liabilities.
- *Lending*. Lenders do not feel that the cash basis generates overly accurate financial statements, and so may refuse to lend money to a business reporting under the cash basis.
- *Audited financial statements*. Auditors will not approve financial statements that were compiled under the cash basis, so a dealership will need to convert to the accrual basis if it wants to have audited statements.
- *Management reporting*. Since the results of cash basis financial statements can be inaccurate, management reports should not be issued that are based upon it.

In short, the numerous problems with the cash basis of accounting may cause an organization to use the accrual basis of accounting.

## The Balance Sheet

In the preceding pages, we addressed how accounting transactions are recorded, and where they are stored. Once these transactions have been stored within the general ledger, they can be summarized into a set of financial statements, which management, lenders, and outside investors can peruse to gain a better idea of the financial condition of the business. The key financial statements are the balance sheet and income statement.

A dealership should produce a *balance sheet* at the end of each reporting period (which is probably on a monthly basis). This report shows the total assets, liabilities, and owners' equity as of the final day of the reporting period. A sample balance sheet appears in the following exhibit.

**Sample Dealership Balance Sheet**

| | |
|---|---:|
| **Assets** | |
| Current assets: | |
| Cash | $250,000 |
| Accounts receivable, net of allowance for doubtful accounts | 750,000 |
| Inventories | 5,500,000 |
| Other current assets | 150,000 |
| Total current assets | 6,650,000 |
| | |
| Property and equipment, net of accumulated depreciation | 4,000,000 |
| Finance receivables, net of allowance for losses | 3,000,000 |
| Other noncurrent assets | 500,000 |
| Total assets | $14,150,000 |
| | |
| **Liabilities and Equity** | |
| Current liabilities: | |
| Floor plan notes payable | $3,000,000 |
| Current maturities of long-term debt | 100,000 |
| Trade payables | 300,000 |
| Accrued liabilities | 250,000 |
| Total current liabilities | 3,650,000 |
| | |
| Long-term debt, less current maturities | 6,500,000 |
| Deferred income taxes | 200,000 |
| Other long-term liabilities | 100,000 |
| Total liabilities | 10,450,000 |
| | |
| Equity: | |
| Common stock | 50,000 |
| Additional paid-in capital | 1,000,000 |
| Retained earnings | 2,650,000 |
| Total stockholders' equity | 3,700,000 |
| Total liabilities and equity | $14,150,000 |

The balance sheet reports the amount of assets, liabilities, and equity. An *asset* is an expenditure that has utility through multiple future reporting periods. If an expenditure does not have such utility, it is instead considered an expense. For example, a dealership pays its electricity bill. This expenditure covers something (electricity) that only had utility during the billing period, which is a past period; therefore, it is recorded as an expense. Conversely, the firm buys a lift, which it expects to use for the next ten years. Since this expenditure has utility through multiple future periods, it is recorded as an asset.

A *liability* is a legally binding obligation payable to another entity. Liabilities are incurred in order to fund the ongoing activities of a business. Examples of liabilities are accounts payable, accrued expenses, wages payable, and taxes payable. These obligations are eventually settled through the transfer of cash or other assets to the other party.

*Equity* is the net amount of funds invested in a dealership by its owners, plus any earnings that have been retained within the business. It is also calculated as the difference between the total of all recorded assets and liabilities on the firm's balance sheet.

## The Income Statement

A dealership needs to produce an *income statement* at the end of each reporting period (which is probably on a monthly basis). This report shows the revenue generated during the reporting period, from which all expenses incurred during that period are subtracted, leaving a profit or loss. An example of an income statement appears in the following exhibit.

## Sample Dealership Income Statement

| Revenues: | |
|---|---:|
| New vehicle retail | $3,900,000 |
| Used vehicle retail | 2,600,000 |
| Used vehicle wholesale | 300,000 |
| Finance and insurance | 350,000 |
| Service, body and parts | 850,000 |
| Fleet and other | 250,000 |
| Total revenues | 8,250,000 |
| | |
| **Cost of Sales:** | |
| New vehicle retail | 3,500,000 |
| Used vehicle retail | 2,400,000 |
| Used vehicle wholesale | 300,000 |
| Service, body and parts | 400,000 |
| Fleet and other | 200,000 |
| Total cost of sales | 6,800,000 |
| Gross profit | 1,450,000 |
| | |
| Selling, general and administrative | 850,000 |
| Depreciation and amortization | 100,000 |
| Operating income | 500,000 |
| | |
| Floor plan interest expense | -50,000 |
| Other interest expense | -60,000 |
| Other income | -10,000 |
| Income before income taxes | 380,000 |
| Income tax provision | 80,000 |
| Net income | $300,000 |

# Profit Center Reporting

A car dealership may have a number of functional areas, such as new car sales, used car sales, servicing, body shop, and parts. That being the case, it makes a great deal of sense to go beyond the basic financial statements (which only report on the entity as a whole) and create profit center reports for each of these areas. A *profit center* is a business unit that generates revenue and profits or losses. A profit center report states the revenue received from operations during a reporting period, and offsets against it all direct costs for the profit center in question. A *direct cost* is one that varies as a result of changes in activity. For example, the parts department will have no offsetting parts costs if there are no sales.

There will also be any number of indirect costs that should be assigned to each profit center. For example, the costs of utilities, janitorial, and rent should certainly be assigned to each profit center, since each one would have to consume these costs if they were operated as separate entities; in this case, the dealership as a whole is paying the bills for expenses that the profit centers would have to consume. The issue is how to allocate these expenses to each profit center. Here are several possibilities:

- Assign rent and utilities based on the square footage occupied by each profit center.
- Assign employee compensation based on where they spend the bulk of their time. For example, the used car lot attendant's wages would be charged to the used cars profit center, while the parts counter's staff wages would be charged to the parts counter.
- Assign employee benefits based on the number of employees working in each profit center (but only those participating in the relevant benefit plans).
- Assign office supplies based on a periodic assessment of which profit centers are using them.
- Assign outside services based on usage. For example, the cost of washing the windows of the showroom would be charged to the new cars profit center, while the cost of inventory taking would be charged to the parts counter.
- Assign the cost of a fidelity bond based on the number of employees in each profit center, since the bond fee is directly linked to the number of employees.

In order to use profit center reporting, revenues and expenses must be assigned to individual profit centers. For example, sales and expenses could be recorded within revenue sub-accounts for Internet sales, new cars, used cars, new trucks, and used trucks. Yet another variation is to record fleet sales separately. Additional profit centers may be set up for parts, paint and body shop, and even vending machines. Clearly, this level of detail calls for a large number of accounts, with many profit center options for each revenue and expense account.

In cases where profit centers do not benefit from an incurred expense (such as the salary of the owner), the related expenses should not be assigned to any profit centers. However, there should be relatively few of these expenses. In most cases, at least one profit center will benefit from an incurred expense, and so should be charged the amount of that expense.

Now that we have addressed the basic structure of and reports generated by an accounting system, we will address the specific transactions that a dealership accountant will likely need to record. The following topics are targeted at transactions unique to dealerships, rather than the more ordinary ones, such as the routine recordation of utilities bills and generic payments to suppliers. The topics begin with sales transactions, which are followed by expense transactions; we then work down through asset, liabilities, equity, and payroll.

## Accounting for Financed Vehicle Sales

A dealership enters into a contract with a lender whenever a customer wants to use a loan from the lender to pay for a vehicle being sold by the dealership. The entry for it is to record a receivable for the contract (since it may take a few days for the lender to forward funds to the dealership), as well as a receivable for the dealership reserve, which is the commission that the dealership earns from the lender in exchange for directing its customer to the lender. Offsetting these receivables are the cost of the vehicle, and any sales taxes and registration fees owed to the government as a result of the sale. A sample entry follows.

**Recordation of Vehicle Sale with Lender Contract**

|  | Debit | Credit |
|---|---|---|
| Contracts in Transit (asset) | 45,000 | |
| Dealership Reserve Receivable (asset) | 300 | |
| Cost of Sales (expense) | 40,000 | |
| Revenue – Vehicles (revenue) | | 41,850 |
| Revenue – Dealership Reserve (revenue) | | 300 |
| Inventory – New Cars (asset) | | 40,000 |
| Sales Taxes Payable (liability) | | 3,000 |
| Registration Fees Payable (liability) | | 150 |

A *contract in transit* is essentially a contract that has been made with the dealership, but has not yet been carried out to the extent that the dealership has been paid. In this case, the money yet to be paid is a contract in transit.

> **Note:** The cost of a vehicle can be found on the factory invoice or the dealership's vehicle inventory record.

The entry changes somewhat if the dealership accepts a trade-in as part of a vehicle sale transaction. In this case, it is accepting a new asset into inventory, and the sales tax payable will decline somewhat, since the tax is only due on the net sale (excluding the trade-in). As an example, the entry in the following exhibit duplicates the immediately preceding one, except that an $8,000 trade-in is included in the entry.

**Recordation of Vehicle Sale with Trade-In**

|  | Debit | Credit |
|---|---|---|
| Contracts in Transit (asset) | 36,500 | |
| Inventory – Used Cars (asset) | 8,000 | |
| Dealership Reserve Receivable (asset) | 300 | |
| Cost of Sales (expense) | 40,000 | |
| Revenue – Vehicles (revenue) | | 41,850 |
| Revenue – Dealership Reserve (revenue) | | 300 |
| Inventory – New Cars (asset) | | 40,000 |
| Sales Taxes Payable (liability) | | 2,500 |
| Registration Fees Payable (liability) | | 150 |

When the lender pays the full amount of the receivable for the preceding transaction, the corresponding entry follows.

**Recordation of Lender Payment on Vehicle Sale**

|  | Debit | Credit |
|---|---|---|
| Cash – Operating (asset) | 45,300 | |
| Contracts in Transit (asset) | | 45,000 |
| Dealership Reserve Receivable (asset) | | 300 |

As part of the month-end closing process, the accountant should itemize all contracts in transit, and contact the lender in regard to any contracts for which payment appears to have been delayed.

# Accounting for Direct Billings

A dealership may sell vehicles to a local government entity, in which case it usually bills the government directly, and must maintain an outstanding receivable until the government pays the invoice. A sample entry follows, where the cost of the related vehicles is also charged to the cost of sales.

**Recordation of Vehicle Billing**

|  | Debit | Credit |
|---|---|---|
| Accounts Receivable (asset) | 70,000 | |
| Cost of Sales (expense) | 67,000 | |
| Revenue – Vehicles (revenue) | | 70,000 |
| Inventory – New Cars (asset) | | 67,000 |

Another scenario is that the dealership issues an invoice to a customer for servicing work, where the customer is expected to pay within a reasonable payment period, such as 30 days. In this case, the accountant creates an account receivable and offsetting sale, as well as a charge of the labor and parts to expense. A sample entry follows, where the receivable amount is the total of the sale generated by the dealership, plus sales tax. The entry also charges the cost of the materials and labor that was used in the servicing work to the cost of sales.

**Recordation of Servicing Work Billing**

|  | Debit | Credit |
|---|---|---|
| Accounts Receivable (asset) | 1,070 | |
| Cost of Sales – Labor (expense) | 300 | |
| Cost of Sales – Materials (expense) | 200 | |
| Revenue – Servicing Labor (revenue) | | 600 |
| Revenue – Servicing Parts (revenue) | | 400 |
| Direct Labor (expense) | | 300 |
| Inventory – Parts (asset) | | 200 |
| Sales Taxes Payable (liability) | | 70 |

When a customer pays for the preceding invoice for servicing work, the required entry is to increase the amount of cash on hand, while reducing the account receivable by an equivalent amount. A sample entry follows.

**Recordation of Customer Payment on Outstanding Receivable**

|  | Debit | Credit |
|---|---|---|
| Cash – Operating (asset) | 1,070 | |
| Accounts Receivable (asset) | | 1,070 |

## Accounting for Quick Service Sales

A dealership may maintain an on-site quick service facility, where customers can go for an oil and filter change. These transactions involve a limited amount of service parts and just a few staff, where all payments are made in cash. The related accounting requires a reduction of the parts inventory and the charging of labor time to the cost of sales. A sample entry follows.

**Recordation of a Quick Service Sale**

| | Debit | Credit |
|---|---|---|
| Cash – Operating (asset) | 40 | |
| Cost of Sales – Quick Service Labor (expense) | 5 | |
| Cost of Sales – Shop Supplies (expense) | 8 | |
|    Inventory – Work-in-Process (asset) | | 5 |
|    Inventory – Shop Supplies (asset) | | 8 |
|    Revenue – Quick Service (revenue) | | 38 |
|    Sales Taxes Payable (liability) | | 2 |

## Accounting for Extended Warranty Sales

The manufacturer may offer extended warranty programs, which the dealership sells to its customers at a markup. The warranties are commonly sold as part of a new car sale, but we are showing the entry for this as though the warranty is sold separately – which clarifies which accounts are used. A sample entry follows, where it is assumed that the dealership incurs a liability to pay the manufacturer for the extended liability (since the manufacturer is providing the warranty coverage).

**Recordation of Extended Warranty Sale**

| | Debit | Credit |
|---|---|---|
| Cash – Operating (asset) | 1,500 | |
| Cost of Sales – Extended Warranty (expense) | 1,000 | |
|    Revenue – Extended Warranties (revenue) | | 1,500 |
|    Accounts Payable (liability) | | 1,000 |

## Accounting for Insurance Commissions

A dealership may have arrangements with a number of insurance companies, where it directs customers to them in exchange for a commission on any insurance policies sold to the customers. A sample entry for such a transaction appears in the following exhibit.

**Recordation of Insurance Commission**

|  | Debit | Credit |
|---|---|---|
| Insurance Commissions Receivable (asset) | 400 |  |
| Other Income – Insurance Commissions (revenue) |  | 400 |

Depending on the level of detail desired, these commissions could be tracked by profit center, such as insurance commissions related to new cars, used cars, and trucks.

When a commission payment is received, it offsets the outstanding receivable pertaining to the matter – as shown in the following exhibit.

**Recordation of Insurance Commission Payment**

|  | Debit | Credit |
|---|---|---|
| Cash – Operating (asset) | 400 |  |
| Insurance Commissions Receivable (asset) |  | 400 |

When there are many commissions due, it can make sense to review the list of unpaid amounts at the end of each month, and make inquiries with insurers regarding any receivables for which payment is overdue.

## Accounting for Warranty Claims

The dealership may have to complete warranty-related repairs on vehicles owned by its customers. This warranty claim is then billed to the manufacturer, who reimburses the dealership. A sample billing transaction appears in the following sample entry.

**Recordation of Warranty Claim**

|  | Debit | Credit |
|---|---|---|
| Accounts Receivable – Warranty Claims (asset) | 1,200 |  |
| Cost of Sales – Warranty Labor (expense) | 400 |  |
| Cost of Sales – Warranty Parts (expense) | 250 |  |
| Inventory – Work-in-Process (asset) |  | 400 |
| Inventory – Parts (asset) |  | 250 |
| Revenue – Warranty Claims (revenue) |  | 1,200 |

Upon review, the manufacturer may not pay the full amount of a claim. If so, the amount not paid should be subtracted from the claim revenue previously recognized by the distributor. The following entry shows how this might be done for an invoice amount of $1,200, where the manufacturer refuses to pay $100.

**Recordation of Manufacturer Short Payment**

|  | Debit | Credit |
|---|---|---|
| Cash – Operating (asset) | 1,100 | |
| Revenue – Warranty Claims (revenue) | 100 | |
| Accounts Receivable – Warranty Claims (asset) | | 1,200 |

## Accounting for New Vehicles

A dealership will take delivery of new vehicles from the factory at regular intervals. When this happens, the accountant records the factory invoice amount for each new car, less the amount of any holdback. The *holdback* concept arises when the manufacturer inflates invoice prices by a predetermined amount (usually two or three percent), and then pays the inflated amount back to the dealership at intervals, such as once a quarter. Holdbacks are used so that the dealership can sell its vehicles at or near invoice, while still making hundreds of dollars on the transaction. In the accounting entry, the holdback amount is recorded as a receivable due from the manufacturer. A sample entry follows.

**Recordation of New Car Purchase from Manufacturer**

|  | Debit | Credit |
|---|---|---|
| Inventory – New Cars (asset) | 45,000 | |
| Accounts Receivable – Holdbacks (asset) | 1,000 | |
| Notes Payable (liability) | | 46,000 |

When the dealership makes a payment to reduce its note payable to the manufacturer while paying off the accrued interest, this reduces the amount of cash left on hand, as noted in the following sample entry.

**Recordation of Payment Against Note Payable**

|  | Debit | Credit |
|---|---|---|
| Notes Payable (liability) | 10,000 | |
| Interest Expense (expense) | 5,000 | |
| Cash – Operating (asset) | | 15,000 |

In cases where the dealership is purchasing a vehicle from another dealership, it is more likely to acquire the vehicle for cash. If so, the credit to notes payable is replaced by a credit to the cash account, showing that the dealership's cash balance has declined. The entry follows.

**Recordation of New Car Purchase from Another Dealership**

| | Debit | Credit |
|---|---|---|
| Inventory – New Cars (asset) | 45,000 | |
| Accounts Receivable – Holdbacks (asset) | 1,000 | |
| Cash – Operating (asset) | | 46,000 |

The dealership may upgrade a purchased vehicle with add-on products. If so, it increases the cost of the vehicle by the cost of the materials and labor added to it. A sample entry follows.

**Recordation of Upgrade to New Car**

| | Debit | Credit |
|---|---|---|
| Inventory – New Cars (asset) | 350 | |
| Inventory – Parts (asset) | | 200 |
| Direct Labor (expense) | | 150 |

**Note:** The accounting for trucks is the same as we have just described for cars. To record these transactions with trucks, just use a separate inventory account, entitled "Inventory – New Trucks," rather than "Inventory – New Cars."

When a new vehicle is acquired, assign it a stock number (typically assigned in straight numerical sequence), so that it can be tracked on the lot. Acquired used cars should be assigned a stock number in the same manner.

## Accounting for Demonstrators

A car dealership will likely set aside a few vehicles for use as demonstrators. Customers drive them short distances as part of their evaluation process for buying a vehicle. There are several entries associated with the accounting for demonstrators, of which the first is a reallocation entry, shifting a demonstrator from the new cars inventory to the demonstrators inventory. A sample entry follows.

**Recordation of Transfer to Demonstrator Inventory**

| | Debit | Credit |
|---|---|---|
| Inventory – Demonstrators (asset) | 45,000 | |
| Inventory – New Cars (asset) | | 45,000 |

The dealership may elect to upgrade a demonstrator. If so, it needs to account for the movement of parts and use of installation labor, which are shifted to the total cost of the demonstrator. A sample entry follows, for the installation of a satellite radio connection.

21

**Recordation of Upgrade to Demonstrator**

| | Debit | Credit |
|---|---|---|
| Inventory – Demonstrators (asset) | 350 | |
| Inventory – Parts (asset) | | 200 |
| Direct Labor (expense) | | 150 |

In addition to the costing entry just noted, a record of all upgrades should be kept on a separate vehicle inventory record, which is used not only to compile the final cost when the vehicle is eventually sold, but also to use as the basis for compiling the price that will be charged for it.

## Accounting for Used Cars

A dealership may maintain only a modest stock of used cars, or it may deal with these vehicles exclusively. When a used car is purchased (typically at auction), the dealership records the purchase price of the vehicle, into which is incorporated the auction fee – it is not broken out separately. An example entry follows.

**Recordation of Used Car Purchase**

| | Debit | Credit |
|---|---|---|
| Inventory – Used Cars (asset) | 22,000 | |
| Notes Payable (liability) | | 22,000 |

Once a used car has been acquired, it is examined for repair issues. All necessary repairs are then made, and the associated charges are billed to the vehicle in question. This reduces the parts inventory and shifts the repair expense to the value of the used car. An example follows.

**Recordation of Repairs to Used Car**

| | Debit | Credit |
|---|---|---|
| Inventory – Used Cars (asset) | 350 | |
| Inventory – Parts (asset) | | 200 |
| Direct Labor (expense) | | 150 |

If a used car has been in inventory for an extended period of time, it may be necessary to write down its book value in the dealership's accounting records. The book value of a used car should be the lower of its cost or its appraised wholesale value. The cost of the vehicle is its purchase price, plus the cost of any upgrades made to it, plus the auction fee on the unit, and any travel expenditures incurred while acquiring it.

A write-down analysis should be conducted at the end of each month. If a write-down is deemed necessary, the accountant debits an adjustment account, which recognizes an immediate loss in the amount of the write-down. This loss is used to reduce the value of the used car in question. An example follows.

**Write-Down of Used Car Value**

|  | Debit | Credit |
|---|---|---|
| Adjustment – Used Car Inventory (loss) | 1,000 | |
| Inventory – Used Cars (asset) | | 1,000 |

Any subsequent sale of a used car involves the same journal entry already noted for the sale of a new vehicle.

> **Note:** The accounting for used trucks is the same as what we just outlined for used cars.

A dealership might not want to deal with a specific used car, or does not do so in general. If so, it may sell the vehicle to a wholesaler. This usually involves the extension of credit to the wholesaler, so a receivable is generated. An example appears in the following entry.

**Recordation of Vehicle Sale to Wholesaler**

|  | Debit | Credit |
|---|---|---|
| Accounts Receivable (asset) | 10,000 | |
| Cost of Sales – Used Cars (expense) | 9,000 | |
| Inventory – Used Cars (asset) | | 9,000 |
| Revenue – Used Cars (revenue) | | 10,000 |

## Accounting for Tires

A dealership will likely maintain a substantial inventory of tires. Since tires can constitute a substantial investment, they are usually tracked within a separate inventory account from parts and accessories. The initial entry to log their acquisition appears in the following exhibit.

**Recordation of Tire Purchases**

|  | Debit | Credit |
|---|---|---|
| Inventory – Tires (asset) | 3,000 | |
| Accounts Payable (liability) | | 3,000 |

The tire inventory should be compared to the accounting records once a month with a physical inventory count. If there are any shortfalls from the book balance, the difference should be written off to the cost of sales, as demonstrated in the following example entry.

**Recordation of Write-Down of Tires**

|  | Debit | Credit |
|---|---|---|
| Cost of Sales (expense) | 250 | |
| Inventory – Tires (asset) | | 250 |

When the dealership sells tires to a customer, this involves a reduction of the tire inventory and the charging of labor to the job, against which is offset a cash sale. This will also trigger the recording of a sales tax liability on the price of the tires sold. A sample entry follows.

**Recordation of Tire Sale**

|  | Debit | Credit |
|---|---|---|
| Cash – Operating (asset) | 790 | |
| Cost of Sales – Tires (expense) | 350 | |
| Cost of Sales – Direct Labor (expense) | 50 | |
| Inventory – Work in Process (asset) | | 50 |
| Inventory – Tires (asset) | | 350 |
| Sales Taxes Payable (liability) | | 40 |
| Revenue – Labor (revenue) | | 50 |
| Revenue – Tires (revenue) | | 700 |

# Accounting for Gas, Oil and Grease

A dealership will likely purchase a significant amount of gas, oil and grease as part of its ongoing operations. Given the likely purchasing volumes, it makes sense to track these transactions within a separate account. A sample purchase of these items appears in the following entry, where the purchase is assumed to have been made on credit.

**Recordation of Gas, Oil and Grease Purchase**

|  | Debit | Credit |
|---|---|---|
| Inventory – Gas, Oil and Grease (asset) | 2,500 | |
| Accounts Payable (liability) | | 2,500 |

These assets may be used internally. If so, it can make more sense to charge these purchases straight to expense in the current reporting period, rather than processing them through an inventory account.

A physical inventory should be regularly conducted for these inventory items. If there is a shortfall, the difference is charged to expense, as shown in the following sample entry.

### Recordation of Inventory Adjustment

| | Debit | Credit |
|---|---|---|
| Cost of Sales (expense) | 20 | |
| Inventory – Gas, Oil and Grease (asset) | | 20 |

### Recordation of Gas, Oil and Grease Sale

| | Debit | Credit |
|---|---|---|
| Cash – Operating (asset) | 26 | |
| Cost of Sales (expense) | 8 | |
| Inventory – Gas, Oil and Grease (asset) | | 8 |
| Sales Tax Payable (liability) | | 1 |
| Revenue – Gas, Oil and Grease (revenue) | | 25 |

## Accounting for the Paint and Body Shop

If a dealership has a paint and body shop, then the accountant needs to track the cost of the materials purchased for this department, as well as the value of the paint and other body shop services sold. In the following sample entry, we note that the items purchased for this account are maintained in a separate inventory account.

### Recordation of Paint and Body Shop Purchases

| | Debit | Credit |
|---|---|---|
| Inventory – Paint and Body Shop (asset) | 1,800 | |
| Accounts Payable (liabilities) | | 1,800 |

When the dealership sells services to a customer for body shop labor, as well as all associated materials, the related journal entry can be quite extensive, for the costs of materials, paint, and labor must be charged to the customer, along with any sales tax that may be applicable. A sample entry follows.

**Recordation of Billing for Paint and Body Shop**

|  | Debit | Credit |
|---|---|---|
| Cash – Operating (asset) | 1,830 | |
| Cost of Sales – Paint and Body Labor (expense) | 600 | |
| Cost of Sales – Paint and Body Parts (expense) | 200 | |
| Inventory – Paint and Body Work-in-Process (asset) | | 600 |
| Inventory – Paint and Body Parts (asset) | | 200 |
| Revenue – Paint and Body Labor (revenue) | | 1,400 |
| Revenue – Paint and Body Parts (revenue) | | 400 |
| Sales Tax Payable (liability) | | 30 |

As was the case with inventory counts in other parts of the dealership, any physical inventory count adjustments are charged to the cost of sales – but in this case, the cost of sales for the paint and body shop.

A dealership might instead choose to farm out paint and body shop work on customer vehicles to a contractor that specializes in this type of work. If so, it must record the billed amount of this work as an increase in subcontracted repairs inventory, as noted in the following sample entry.

**Recordation of Billing on Subcontracted Work**

|  | Debit | Credit |
|---|---|---|
| Inventory – Subcontracted Repairs | 800 | |
| Accounts Payable (liability) | | 800 |

Once a customer's car has been returned by the contractor, the dealership can bill the customer for the work, which may include a sales tax charge. A sample entry follows.

**Recordation of Billed Subcontracted Work**

|  | Debit | Credit |
|---|---|---|
| Cash – Operating (asset) | 1,100 | |
| Cost of Sales – Subcontracted Repairs (expense) | 650 | |
| Inventory – Subcontracted Repairs (asset) | | 650 |
| Revenue – Subcontracted Repairs (revenue) | | 1,030 |
| Sales Taxes Payable (liability) | | 70 |

It can be useful to prepare an analysis at the end of each month, showing the cost of each subcontracted repair that has not yet been billed to a customer. This can be useful for spotting delayed billing situations, where the customer needs to be contacted regarding payment.

## Accounting for Work-in-Process

In several of the preceding sample entries, we have noted the use of an Inventory – Work-in-Process account. This account contains the compensation of the dealership's mechanical and body shop technicians that has not yet been billed to any customers. The basic entry to record this labor is noted in the following sample entry. In the entry, not all of the compensation expense incurred by the dealership is charged to work-in-process. Some of it is charged to expense at once as sick time or vacation time, so that only billable time is capitalized into work-in-process.

**Recordation of Work-in-Process Labor**

|  | Debit | Credit |
| --- | --- | --- |
| Inventory – Work-in-Process (asset) | 3,200 | |
| Sick Time (expense) | 200 | |
| Vacation Time (expense) | 600 | |
| Wages – Body Shop (expense) | | 4,000 |

If a customer were to only purchase services involving nothing but labor, then the accounting entry would be to shift the cost of this labor out of the work-in-process asset account and into the cost of sales, as noted in the following sample entry.

**Recordation of Labor Services Sold to Customer**

|  | Debit | Credit |
| --- | --- | --- |
| Cash – Operating (asset) | 500 | |
| Cost of Sales – Work-in-Process (expense) | 300 | |
| Inventory – Work-in-Process (asset) | | 300 |
| Revenue – Labor (revenue) | | 500 |

There will be cases in which some portion of the labor expended cannot be charged to customers. When this is the case, the labor should be charged to expense at once, so that it is no longer reported as an asset. The following sample entry shows how to deal with this issue.

**Write-Off of Unbilled Labor Costs**

|  | Debit | Credit |
| --- | --- | --- |
| Cost of Sales – Work-in-Process (expense) | 450 | |
| Inventory – Work-in-Process (asset) | | 450 |

It may be useful to track work-in-process labor for each profit center within the dealership. Doing so is more complicated from an accounting perspective, but yields better insights into how well each profit center is performing.

## Accounting for Parts and Accessories

A dealership will routinely purchase a large quantity of parts from its suppliers. These purchases are made on credit, so the offset to the receipt of parts and accessories is a credit to the accounts payable account. If the dealership buys in quantity, it may also receive a discount on its acquisition. A sample entry follows.

**Recordation of Parts and Accessories Purchase**

|  | Debit | Credit |
|---|---|---|
| Inventory – Parts and Accessories (asset) | 750 | |
| Accounts Payable (liability) | | 750 |

The dealership's staff should conduct a periodic inventory count to verify whether the inventory stated in its records matches what is on the shelf. When this is not the case, it is usually because the on-hand amount is less than the recorded quantity. If so, the accountant must record a write-off of the cost of the missing items. A sample entry follows.

**Recordation of Write-Down of Parts and Accessories**

|  | Debit | Credit |
|---|---|---|
| Cost of Sales (expense) | 80 | |
| Inventory – Parts and Accessories (asset) | | 80 |

It may also be necessary to write down the carrying amount of the parts and accessories inventory if the market value of any item declines below its recorded cost. The adjustment should result in the market value of an item now being recorded at its carrying amount.

> **Tip:** You may want to subdivide the Cost of Sales accounts into sub-accounts, if you want to track costs in more detail. For example, there could be Cost of Sales – New Cars, Cost of Sales – Used Cars, Cost of Sales – Trucks, and Cost of Sales – Parts and Accessories.

A dealership may sell parts directly to customers through its parts counter. If so, the parts counter can be set up as a separate profit center. A sample entry for a parts counter sale follows.

## Recordation of Parts Counter Sale

|  | Debit | Credit |
|---|---|---|
| Cash – Operating (asset) | 83 | |
| Cost of Sales – Parts Counter (expense) | 40 | |
| Inventory – Parts (asset) | | 40 |
| Sales Taxes Payable (liability) | | 3 |
| Revenue – Parts Counter (revenue) | | 80 |

The parts staff may occasionally find that certain parts held in stock have become obsolete. If so, these parts should be written off to expense in the period when they are determined to be obsolete. A sample entry follows.

## Recordation of Parts Write-Off

|  | Debit | Credit |
|---|---|---|
| Cost of Sales – Parts (expense) | 150 | |
| Inventory – Parts (asset) | | 150 |

Rather than writing off obsolete parts to the cost of sales, another option is to write off parts to a separate account that is designed specifically for write-off expenses. The advantage of doing so is that the cost of write-offs will then be clearly identifiable, rather than being buried within the cost of sales.

# Accounting for Dealership Expenses

The accountant must deal with a variety of standard expenses found in most types of businesses, but there are also some unique ones that are specific to car dealerships. We make note of the issues pertaining to these more unusual expenses in the following sub-sections, presented in alphabetical order.

### Advertising Expense

A dealership will likely spend considerable amounts on advertising expense. This may encompass television and radio ads, as well as billboards, direct mail pieces, and other forms of direct advertising. It may also sponsor local sport teams and other events, while also giving away a variety of themed paraphernalia, such as key fobs and coffee cups. All of these expenditures are charged to expense through the advertising expense account.

### Contracted Services Expense

A dealership may rely on a number of third-party providers to handle a variety of specialized tasks on its behalf. For example, it may contract with outsiders for landscaping, janitorial, trash removal, snow removal, collections, armored car service, and shopper surveys. All of these expenditures can be charged to expense through the contracted services expense account.

### Dealership Vehicle Expense

A dealership may have an abundance of demonstrators and company vehicles, all of which must be serviced from time to time. The cost of the labor and parts used during periodic servicing, as well as any car washes and gasoline refills, licensing and registration are charged to the dealership vehicle expense account.

### Delivery Expense

All expenses incurred to prepare a vehicle for delivery to a customer are included in the Delivery Expense account. Examples of the costs that might be charged to this account include:

- Filling the tank with gasoline
- Delivery labor (when vehicles are delivered to customer locations)
- Detailing labor
- Detailing supplies consumed
- Safety inspection labor
- Removal of unwanted accessories

### Equipment Repairs Expense

A dealership has a substantial investment in equipment, which will require repairs from time to time. For example, a lift in a service bay may need to be repaired, as might a copier machine in the accounting department. The cost of these repairs should be charged to the equipment repairs expense account.

### Floorplan Interest Expense

Dealerships may maintain substantial amounts of vehicle inventory on their lots, so that prospective customers can view the vehicles. These vehicles are financed with asset-backed loans, known as *floorplan loans*, which are provided by banks, specialty lenders, and vehicle manufacturers. Under asset-backed loan arrangements, the debt must be paid back when the underlying vehicle is sold. For the period when a vehicle has not yet been sold, the dealership must pay floorplan interest expense to the lender. This charge can be substantial.

> **Note:** Given the potential size of floorplan interest charges by the lender, it can make sense to reconcile the lender's monthly statements to the dealership's internal records to see if there are any discrepancies.

When a dealership enters into a floorplan arrangement with a vehicle manufacturer, the manufacturer can issue a credit to offset the floorplan interest charges, thereby encouraging the dealership to acquire more vehicles from it.

## Miscellaneous Supplies Expense

A dealership will inevitably consume a fair amount of miscellaneous supplies during the ongoing conduct of operations, such as paper mats used in cars while they are being serviced, or small tools. While these costs can usually be charged to a specific profit center, it is not usually cost-effective to charge them to a specific customer sale. Instead, they are charged to the miscellaneous supplies expense account.

## Policy Work

A dealership might decide to provide occasional services or parts to customers for free, in order to maintain high levels of customer satisfaction. This is especially common when customers have complaints about service work or the quality of parts purchased from the dealership. In these situations, not only does the customer not pay, but the dealership also has no expectation of billing the manufacturer for the costs incurred. Instead, these costs are charged to expense. Examples of policy work are fixing minor rattles, buffing out minor scratches, and replacing worn parts on a used car shortly after the customer takes delivery.

## Repossession Losses

A dealership may need to repossess new or used vehicles, due to the nonpayment of loans by customers. The cost of these repossessions is derived from the loss in value on the repossessed vehicles. The dealership may charge these costs to expense only as incurred, or set up a reserve and charge an estimated amount to the reserve in each reporting period, based on its history of repossession losses.

# Accounting for Petty Cash

A dealer may maintain a small reserve of cash on hand, which the accountant uses to pay for small expenditures or reimburse employees for amounts that are too small to warrant the issuance of a check.

There are two key transactions associated with a petty cash fund, which are its initial creation and subsequent replenishments. The following entry shows the initial establishment of a petty cash fund with money from the main cash account, which is being established at a $300 funding level.

### Establishment of Petty Cash Fund

|  | Debit | Credit |
|---|---|---|
| Petty Cash (asset) | 300 |  |
| Cash – Operating (asset) |  | 300 |

Petty cash will thereafter be used to make a variety of small payments, each of which is logged by the petty cash custodian. When the residual amount of cash in the account runs low, it is time to replenish the fund. This is done by summarizing the log of expenditures and formally recording them in the accounting system.

### Recordation of Petty Cash Disbursements

|  | Debit | Credit |
|---|---|---|
| Travel and Entertainment Expense (expense) | 190 |  |
| Postage Expense (expense) | 20 |  |
| Delivery Expense (expense) | 35 |  |
| Office Supplies Expense (expense) | 5 |  |
| Cash – Operating (asset) |  | 250 |

In effect, the initial balance at which the petty cash fund is established is what is always stated on the books of the dealership. Any replenishments of the fund are intended to maintain that initial funding level.

## Accounting for Dealership Cash Receipts

There are a number of cases in which a dealership might receive cash, such as from vending machines, parts customers, and customers making initial payments on the purchase of a vehicle. To demonstrate how one of these transactions could be recorded, the following entry shows the recordation for vending machine receipts.

### Recordation of Vending Machine Receipts

|  | Debit | Credit |
|---|---|---|
| Cash – Operating (asset) | 75 |  |
| Other Income - Vending (revenue) |  | 75 |

As another example, the following entry shows the recordation for a check payment from a customer who has purchased automotive parts.

### Recordation of Parts Purchase by Customer

|  | Debit | Credit |
|---|---|---|
| Cash – Operating (asset) | 280 |  |
| Revenue – Service and Parts (revenue) |  | 280 |

Finally, it is quite likely that the buyer of a new vehicle will be required to pay a down payment at the point of purchase. The following entry shows this transaction.

### Recordation of Down Payment on Vehicle Purchase

|  | Debit | Credit |
|---|---|---|
| Cash – Operating (assets) | 2,000 |  |
| Revenue – Vehicles (revenue) |  | 2,000 |

A dealership may receive a substantial amount of funds from its customers each day, so the accountant must ensure that a delivery of all cash and checks is made to the bank at the end of every business day.

Most of the vehicle sales made by a dealership will probably be on credit, where a lender is extending credit to the customer, and forwarding funds to the dealership. These arrangements are initially classified as a receivable by the dealership, and then shifted into the cash account once the lender forwards a payment to the dealership. An example of such a payment is shown in the following entry.

**Recordation of Payment by Lender for Contract in Transit**

|  | Debit | Credit |
|---|---|---|
| Cash – Operating (asset) | 30,000 | |
|    Contracts in Transit (asset) | | 30,000 |

A dealership will routinely make many payments to its suppliers. These are recorded as cash disbursements from the operating cash account. The entry is a reduction of the accounts payable account, as well as the cash account, since assets are being used to settle obligations. A sample entry for a daily check run to pay suppliers appears in the following exhibit.

**Recordation of Check Run to Pay Suppliers**

|  | Debit | Credit |
|---|---|---|
| Accounts Payable (liability) | 16,215 | |
|    Cash – Operating (asset) | | 16,215 |

## Accounting for Factory Receivables

When a new vehicle is purchased from the factory, the manufacturer may overbill the sale price of the car and rebate it back to the dealership periodically. This is classified as a holdback, and can sum to a substantial amount. Given the size of this receivable, it can make sense to record it separately from the other trade accounts receivable, in an Accounts Receivable – Holdbacks account. The dealership may also be due a co-operative advertising payment from the factory, which might be recorded within an Accounts Receivable – Cooperative Advertising account. *Cooperative advertising* is a cost sharing arrangement to pay for advertising. Under this agreement, the factory agrees to compensate its distributors for a certain proportion of the advertising and promotion costs related to their sale of the factory's products. An example of the entry used for the recordation of a cooperative advertising arrangement appears in the following entry.

### Recordation of Cooperative Advertising Receivable

|  | Debit | Credit |
|---|---|---|
| Accounts Receivable – Cooperative Advertising (asset) | 2,300 | |
| Advertising Expense (expense) | | 2,300 |

The accountant should reconcile the unpaid balance of any holdbacks to the factory's statement, to ensure that the dealership is paid the full amount it is expecting. Any holdbacks that the factory refuses to pay must be written off.

Another scenario involving factory receivables is when the factory mandates that the dealership inspect each vehicle delivered to it. If so, the dealership may be able to charge the cost of this inspection labor back to the factory. A sample entry follows.

### Recordation of New Vehicle Inspection Labor

|  | Debit | Credit |
|---|---|---|
| Accounts Receivable – Factory (asset) | 100 | |
| Cost of Sales – New Vehicle Inspection (expense) | 30 | |
| Inventory – Work-in-Process (asset) | | 30 |
| Revenue – New Vehicle Inspections (revenue) | | 100 |

## Accounting for Notes Receivable

A dealership might elect to offer financing to its customers directly, rather than outsourcing this service to a third-party lender. If so, the initial transaction is to record a cash down payment, note receivable, finance charge, registration fee, sales tax, and so forth, while also charging the cost of the vehicle to the cost of sales. A sample entry follows.

### Recordation of Dealership Financing of Vehicle Sale

|  | Debit | Credit |
|---|---|---|
| Cash – Operating (asset) | 1,000 | |
| Notes Receivable (asset) | 39,000 | |
| Cost of Sales (expense) | 37,000 | |
| Revenue – Vehicles (revenue) | | 36,050 |
| Revenue – Finance Fee (revenue) | | 1,000 |
| Inventory – New Cars (asset) | | 37,000 |
| Sales Taxes Payable (liability) | | 2,800 |
| Registration Fees Payable (liability) | | 150 |

When the customer submits a payment to the dealership, this reduces the amount of the note receivable, as shown in the following entry.

## Recordation of Customer Payment on Note Receivable

|  | Debit | Credit |
|---|---|---|
| Cash – Operating (asset) | 500 |  |
| Notes Receivable (asset) |  | 500 |

# Accounting for Doubtful Accounts

If the decision is made to offer sales to customers on credit, it is quite likely that some invoices will never be paid. If so, the accountant must write off these invoices as bad debts. There are two ways to do so, which are covered in this section under the headings of the direct write-off method and the allowance for doubtful accounts.

### Direct Write-Off Method

The direct write-off method is the practice of charging bad debts to expense in the period when individual invoices have been clearly identified as bad debts. The specific activity needed to write off an account receivable under this method is to create a credit memo for the customer in question, which exactly offsets the amount of the bad debt. Creating the credit memo will require a debit to a bad debt expense account and a credit to the accounts receivable account.

The method does not involve a reduction in the amount of recorded sales, only an increase of the bad debt expense. For example, a dealership records a sale on credit of $1,000 for body shop work, and records it with a debit to the accounts receivable account and a credit to the revenue account. After two months, the customer is only able to pay $800 of the open balance, so the firm must write off $200. It does so with a $200 credit to the accounts receivable account and an offsetting debit to the bad debt expense account. Thus, the revenue amount remains the same, the remaining receivable is eliminated, and an expense is created in the amount of the bad debt.

The direct write off method delays the recognition of expenses related to a revenue-generating transaction, and so is considered an excessively aggressive accounting method, since it makes a dealership appear more profitable in the short term than it really is. For example, it may recognize $50,000 in revenue in one period, and then wait three or four months to collect all of the related accounts receivable before finally charging some items off to the bad debt expense. This creates a lengthy delay between revenue recognition and the recognition of expenses that are directly related to that revenue. Thus, the profit in the initial month is overstated, while profit is understated in the month when the bad debts are finally charged to expense.

The direct write off method can be considered a reasonable accounting method if the amount that is written off is immaterial, since doing so has a minimal impact on a dealership's reported financial results.

### Allowance for Doubtful Accounts

The allowance for doubtful accounts is a reduction of the total amount of accounts receivable appearing on the balance sheet. This allowance represents the accountant's best estimate of the amount of accounts receivable that will not be paid in the future by customers.

If the dealership is using the accrual basis of accounting, it should record an allowance for doubtful accounts, since this approach provides an estimate of future bad debts that improves the accuracy of the financial statements. Also, by recording the allowance at the same time it records a sale, the accountant can properly match the projected bad debt expense against the related sale in the same period, which provides a more accurate view of the true profitability of a sale.

For example, a dealership records $30,000 of parts sales to a number of customers, and projects (based on historical experience) that it will incur 1% of this amount as bad debts, though it does not know exactly which customers will default. It records the 1% of projected bad debts as a $300 debit to the bad debt expense account and a $300 credit to the allowance for doubtful accounts. The bad debt expense is charged to expense right away, and the allowance for doubtful accounts becomes a reserve account that offsets the account receivable of $30,000 (for a net receivable outstanding of $29,700).

Later, a customer defaults on an invoice totaling $200. Accordingly, the accountant credits the accounts receivable account by $200 to reduce the amount of outstanding accounts receivable, and debits the allowance for doubtful accounts by $200. This entry reduces the balance in the allowance account to $100. The entry does not impact earnings in the current period.

---

**Note:** No matter which method is used, a dealership might eventually receive late payment on a debt that it had already written off. This reverses the original account write-off. Under the direct write-off method, the result will be an immediate reduction in the amount of bad debt expense. Under the allowance for doubtful accounts method, the result will be an increase in the allowance for doubtful accounts.

---

## Accounting for Insurance Claims

What about cases in which the vehicles owned by a dealership are damaged in road accidents, perhaps during test drives? When this happens, the dealership files a claim with its insurance company. However, no receivable is recorded until the amount of the insurance payment can be reasonably ascertained, and the payment is probable.

## Accounting for Other Automotive Assets

Depending on the nature of the dealership, it might occasionally acquire other assets than cars and trucks. For example, it might purchase a motorcycle or a camper van. If these purchases are rare, they can be made into an Inventory – Other Automotive account, using the various purchase and sale journal entries already noted for new cars. However, if the dealership engages in substantial sales volume for these items, it could use a separate account for each one, such as:

- Inventory – Boats
- Inventory – Camper Vans

- Inventory – Farm Tractors
- Inventory – Golf Carts
- Inventory – Motorcycles
- Inventory – Scooters
- Inventory – Snowmobiles

## Accounting for Prepaid Insurance

A dealership will need to pay for commercial property insurance and workers compensation insurance, as well as garage keepers insurance. The last of these policies is unique to dealerships and similar entities, and provides them with liability protection in the event of a customer's vehicle being damaged while in the dealership's possession for repairs, bodywork, or storage. These and other types of insurance are paid in advance of the coverage period, which means that they are initially treated as a short-term asset. The amounts paid are then charged to expense over the coverage period. A sample entry for the purchase of prepaid insurance appears in the following exhibit.

**Recordation of Prepaid Insurance Payment**

|  | Debit | Credit |
|---|---|---|
| Prepaid Insurance (asset) | 5,000 | |
| Cash – Operating (asset) | | 5,000 |

When this insurance asset is charged to expense, the accountant may elect to do so within a single overall monthly charge, or by apportioning the charge among the various profit centers. For example, workers compensation insurance could be apportioned based on the number of employees in each profit center, while garage keepers insurance could be apportioned based on the aggregate retail value of the customer-owned vehicles held by each profit center.

## Accounting for Fixed Assets

A dealership will need to invest in a substantial amount of fixed assets, including more land than most businesses need, landscaping, the dealership building, diagnostic equipment, tire machines, hoists, cabinets, overhead racks, tool racks, jacks, display cases, telephone systems, copiers, and so forth. Given the importance of this asset class, we provide an expanded treatment of the accounting for fixed assets in this section, including the range of possible classifications, depreciation concepts, asset disposals, and the related accounting entries.

### Fixed Asset Classifications

If an expenditure qualifies as a fixed asset, it must be recorded within an account classification. Account classifications are used to aggregate fixed assets into groups, so that the same depreciation methods and useful lives can be applied to them.

37

You also usually create general ledger accounts by classification, and store fixed asset transactions within the classifications to which they belong. Here are the most common classifications used:

- *Buildings*. This account may include the cost of acquiring a building, or the cost of constructing one. If the purchase price of a building includes the cost of land, apportion some of the cost to the Land account (which is not depreciated).
- *Computer equipment*. This classification can include a broad array of computer equipment, such as routers, servers, and backup power generators. It is useful to set the capitalization limit[1] higher than the cost of desktop and laptop computers, so that an excessive number of these assets are not tracked.
- *Equipment*. This category includes all types of diagnostic equipment, hoists, jacks, and so forth.
- *Furniture and fixtures*. This is one of the broadest categories of fixed assets, since it can include such diverse assets as office cubicles and desks.
- *Intangible assets*. This is a non-physical asset, examples of which are trademarks, customer lists, and patented technology.
- *Land*. This is the only asset that is not depreciated, because it is considered to have an indeterminate useful life. Include in this category all expenditures to prepare the land for its intended purpose, such as demolishing an existing building, or grading the land.
- *Land improvements*. Include any expenditures that add functionality to a parcel of land, such as irrigation systems, fencing, and landscaping.
- *Leasehold improvements*. These are improvements to leased space that are made by the tenant, and typically include office space, air conditioning, telephone wiring, and related permanent fixtures.
- *Office equipment*. This account contains such equipment as copiers, printers, and video equipment.
- *Software*. Includes larger types of dealership-wide software, such as a repair scheduling system.
- *Vehicles*. This account contains automobiles, trucks, and similar types of rolling stock.

### Initial Measurement of a Fixed Asset

Initially record a fixed asset at the historical cost of acquiring it, which includes the costs to bring it to the condition and location necessary for its intended use. If these preparatory activities will occupy a period of time, also include in the cost of the asset the interest costs related to the cost of the asset during the preparation period.

---

[1] The capitalization limit is the amount paid for an asset, above which it is recorded as a long-term asset. If the amount paid is less than the capitalization limit, then the amount paid is instead charged to expense in the period incurred.

The activities involved in bringing a fixed asset to the condition and location necessary for its intended purpose include the following:

- Physical construction of the asset
- Demolition of any preexisting structures
- Renovating a preexisting structure to alter it for use by the buyer
- Administrative and technical activities during preconstruction for such activities as designing the asset and obtaining permits
- Administrative and technical work after construction commences for such activities as litigation, labor disputes, and technical problems

## Depreciation Concepts

The purpose of *depreciation* is to charge to expense a portion of an asset that relates to the revenue generated by that asset. This is called the matching principle, where revenues and expenses both appear in the income statement in the same reporting period, which gives the best view of how well a dealership has performed in a given accounting period. The trouble with this matching concept is that there is usually only a tenuous connection between the generation of revenue and a specific asset.

To get around this linkage problem, we usually assume a steady rate of depreciation over the useful life of each asset, so that we approximate a linkage between the recognition of revenues and expenses. This approximation threatens our credulity even more when a dealership uses accelerated depreciation, since the main reason for using it is to defer taxes (and not to better match revenues and expenses).

If we were not to use depreciation at all, we would be forced to charge all assets to expense as soon as we buy them. This would result in large losses in the months when the purchase transaction occurs, followed by unusually high profitability in those periods when the corresponding amount of revenue is recognized, with no off-setting expense. Thus, a dealership that does not use depreciation will have front-loaded expenses, and extremely variable financial results.

There are three factors to consider in the calculation of depreciation, which are as follows:

- *Useful life.* This is the time period over which it is expected that an asset will be productive. Past an asset's useful life, it is no longer cost-effective to continue operating the asset, so a dealership would dispose of it or stop using it. Depreciation is recognized over the useful life of an asset.
- *Salvage value.* When a dealership eventually disposes of an asset, it may be able to sell the asset for some reduced amount, which is the salvage value. Depreciation is calculated based on the asset cost, less any estimated salvage value. If salvage value is expected to be quite small, it is generally ignored for the purpose of calculating depreciation.

---

**EXAMPLE**

The Masterson dealership buys a company car for $40,000 and estimates that its salvage value will be $10,000 in five years, when it plans to dispose of the car. This means that Masterson will depreciate $30,000 of the asset cost over five years, leaving $10,000 of the cost remaining at the end of that time. Masterson expects to then sell the car for $10,000, which will eliminate it from the firm's accounting records.

---

- *Depreciation method.* Depreciation expense can be calculated using an accelerated depreciation method, or evenly over the useful life of the asset. The advantage of using an accelerated method is that you can recognize more depreciation early in the life of a fixed asset, which defers some income tax expense recognition to a later period. The advantage of using a steady depreciation rate is the ease of calculation. An example of an accelerated depreciation method is the MACRS method (as described later). The primary method for steady depreciation is the straight-line method.

## The Straight-Line Method

Under the straight-line method, you would depreciate an asset at the same standard rate throughout its useful life. To do so, recognize depreciation expense evenly over the estimated useful life of an asset. The straight-line calculation steps are:

1. Subtract the estimated salvage value of the asset from the amount at which it is recorded on the books.
2. Determine the estimated useful life of the asset. It is easiest to use a standard useful life for each class of assets.
3. Divide the estimated useful life (in years) into 1 to arrive at the straight-line depreciation rate.
4. Multiply the depreciation rate by the asset cost (less salvage value).

---

**EXAMPLE**

The Higgins Automotive dealership purchases a diagnostic machine for $6,000. It has an estimated salvage value of $1,000 and a useful life of five years. The accountant calculates the annual straight-line depreciation for the machine as follows:

1. Purchase cost of $6,000 – Estimated salvage value of $1,000 = Depreciable asset cost of $5,000
2. 1 ÷ 5-Year useful life = 20% Depreciation rate per year
3. 20% Depreciation rate × $5,000 Depreciable asset cost = $1,000 Annual depreciation

---

## MACRS Depreciation

MACRS depreciation is the tax depreciation system used in the United States. MACRS is an acronym for Modified Accelerated Cost Recovery System. Under MACRS, fixed assets are assigned to a specific asset class. The Internal Revenue Service has published a complete set of depreciation tables for each of these classes. The classes are noted in the following table. Those assets that may be found in a dealership have been stated in bold.

## MACRS Table

| Class | Depreciation Period | Description |
|---|---|---|
| 3-year property | 3 years | Tractor units for over-the-road use, race horses over 2 years old when placed in service, any other horse over 12 years old when placed in service, qualified rent-to-own property |
| 5-year property | 5 years | **Automobiles**, taxis, buses, **trucks, computers and peripheral equipment, office equipment,** any property used in research and experimentation, breeding cattle and dairy cattle, appliances and etc. used in residential rental real estate activity, certain green energy property |
| 7-year property | 7 years | **Office furniture and fixtures,** agricultural machinery and equipment, any property not designated as being in another class, natural gas gathering lines |
| 10-year property | 10 years | Vessels, barges, tugs, single-purpose agricultural or horticultural structures, trees/vines bearing fruits or nuts, qualified small electric meter and smart electric grid systems |
| 15-year property | 15 years | Certain **land improvements** (such as shrubbery, fences, roads, sidewalks and bridges), retail motor fuel outlets, municipal wastewater treatment plants, clearing and grading land improvements for gas utility property, electric transmission property, natural gas distribution lines |
| 20-year property | 20 years | Farm buildings (other than those noted under 10-year property), municipal sewers not categorized as 25-year property, the initial clearing and grading of land for electric utility transmission and distribution plants |
| 25-year property | 25 years | Property that is an integral part of the water distribution facilities, municipal sewers |
| Residential rental property | 27.5 years | Any building or structure where 80% or more of its gross rental income is from dwelling units |
| Nonresidential real property | 39 years | An office building, store, or warehouse that is not residential property or has a class life of less than 27.5 years |

The depreciation rates associated with the more common asset classes are noted in the following exhibit.

**Depreciation Rates for MACRS Asset Classes**

| Recovery Year | 3-Year Property | 5-Year Property | 7-Year Property | 10-Year Property | 15-Year Property | 20-Year Property |
|---|---|---|---|---|---|---|
| 1 | 33.33% | 20.00% | 14.29% | 10.00% | 5.00% | 3.750% |
| 2 | 44.45% | 32.00% | 24.49% | 18.00% | 9.50% | 7.219% |
| 3 | 14.81% | 19.20% | 17.49% | 14.40% | 8.55% | 6.677% |
| 4 | 7.41% | 11.52% | 12.49% | 11.52% | 7.70% | 6.177% |
| 5 |  | 11.52% | 8.93% | 9.22% | 6.93% | 5.713% |
| 6 |  | 5.76% | 8.92% | 7.37% | 6.23% | 5.285% |
| 7 |  |  | 8.93% | 6.55% | 5.90% | 4.888% |
| 8 |  |  | 4.46% | 6.55% | 5.90% | 4.522% |
| 9 |  |  |  | 6.56% | 5.91% | 4.462% |
| 10 |  |  |  | 6.55% | 5.90% | 4.461% |
| 11 |  |  |  | 3.28% | 5.91% | 4.462% |
| 12 |  |  |  |  | 5.90% | 4.461% |
| 13 |  |  |  |  | 5.91% | 4.462% |
| 14 |  |  |  |  | 5.90% | 4.461% |
| 15 |  |  |  |  | 5.91% | 4.462% |
| 16 |  |  |  |  | 2.95% | 4.461% |
| 17 |  |  |  |  |  | 4.462% |
| 18 |  |  |  |  |  | 4.461% |
| 19 |  |  |  |  |  | 4.462% |
| 20 |  |  |  |  |  | 4.461% |
| 21 |  |  |  |  |  | 2.231% |

Depreciation is calculated for tax reporting purposes by aggregating assets into the various classes noted in the preceding exhibit and using the depreciation rates for each class. MACRS ignores salvage value.

The MACRS depreciation rates are used to determine the depreciation expense for taxable income, while other depreciation methods are used to arrive at the depreciation expense for net income. Since these depreciation methods have differing results, there will be a temporary difference between the book values of fixed assets under the two methods, which will gradually be resolved over their useful lives.

### Accounting for Leasehold Improvements

Some dealerships lease space from a third party, and then pay to build out the property with walls, air conditioning, telephone wiring, and related permanent fixtures. These improvements are known as leasehold improvements. In accounting, a leasehold improvement is considered an asset of the tenant if the tenant paid for it, the investment exceeds the capitalization limit of the tenant, and the improvements will be usable for more than one reporting period. If so, you (the tenant) record the investment as a fixed asset and amortize it over the lesser of the remaining term of the lease or the useful life of the improvements. Upon the termination of the lease, all leasehold improvements become the property of the landlord.

## Depreciation Accounting Entries

The basic depreciation entry is to debit the depreciation expense account (which appears in the income statement) and credit the accumulated depreciation account (which appears in the balance sheet as an account that reduces the amount of fixed assets). Over time, the accumulated depreciation balance will continue to increase as more depreciation is added to it, until such time as it equals the original cost of the asset. At that time, stop recording any depreciation expense, since the cost of the asset has now been reduced to zero.

The journal entry for depreciation can be a simple two-line entry designed to accommodate all types of fixed assets, or it may be subdivided into separate entries for each type of fixed asset.

---

**EXAMPLE**

Pembroke Automotive calculates that it should have $25,000 of depreciation expense in the current month. The entry is:

|  | Debit | Credit |
|---|---|---|
| Depreciation Expense (expense) | 25,000 | |
| Accumulated Depreciation (contra asset) | | 25,000 |

In the following month, Pembroke's accountant decides to show a higher level of precision at the expense account level, and instead elects to apportion the $25,000 of depreciation among different expense accounts, so that each class of asset has a separate depreciation charge. The entry is:

|  | Debit | Credit |
|---|---|---|
| Depreciation Expense – Automobiles (expense) | 4,000 | |
| Depreciation Expense – Computer Equipment (expense) | 8,000 | |
| Depreciation Expense – Furniture and Fixtures (expense) | 6,000 | |
| Depreciation Expense – Office Equipment (expense) | 5,000 | |
| Depreciation Expense – Software (expense) | 2,000 | |
| Accumulated Depreciation (contra asset) | | 25,000 |

---

The journal entry to record the amortization of intangible assets is fundamentally the same as the entry for depreciation, except that the accounts used substitute the word "amortization" for depreciation.

---

**EXAMPLE**

Pembroke Automotive calculates that it should have $4,000 of amortization expense in the current month that is related to intangible assets. The entry is:

|  | Debit | Credit |
|---|---|---|
| Amortization Expense (expense) | 4,000 | |
|    Accumulated Amortization (contra asset) | | 4,000 |

---

## Accumulated Depreciation

When you sell or otherwise dispose of an asset, remove all related accumulated depreciation from the accounting records at the same time. Otherwise, an unusually large amount of accumulated depreciation will build up on the balance sheet.

---

**EXAMPLE**

Penn Central Automotive has $1,000,000 of fixed assets, for which it has charged $380,000 of accumulated depreciation. This results in the following presentation on Penn Central's balance sheet:

| | |
|---|---|
| Fixed assets | $1,000,000 |
|   Less: Accumulated depreciation | (380,000) |
| Net fixed assets | $620,000 |

Penn Central then sells a diagnostic machine for $80,000 that had an original cost of $140,000, and for which it had already recorded accumulated depreciation of $50,000. It records the sale with this journal entry:

|  | Debit | Credit |
|---|---|---|
| Cash – Operating (asset) | 80,000 | |
| Accumulated Depreciation (contra asset) | 50,000 | |
| Loss on Asset Sale (loss) | 10,000 | |
|    Fixed Assets (asset) | | 140,000 |

As a result of this entry, Penn Central's balance sheet presentation of fixed assets has changed, so that fixed assets before accumulated depreciation have declined to $860,000, and accumulated depreciation has declined to $330,000. The new presentation is:

| | |
|---|---|
| Fixed assets | $860,000 |
|   Less: Accumulated depreciation | (330,000) |
| Net fixed assets | $530,000 |

The amount of net fixed assets declined by $90,000 as a result of the asset sale, which is the sum of the $80,000 cash proceeds and the $10,000 loss resulting from the asset sale.

## Asset Disposal Accounting

There are two scenarios under which you may dispose of a fixed asset. The first situation arises when a fixed asset is being eliminated without receiving any payment in return. This is a common situation when a fixed asset is being scrapped because it is obsolete or no longer in use, and there is no resale market for it. In this case, reverse any accumulated depreciation and reverse the original asset cost. If the asset is fully depreciated, that is the extent of the entry.

### EXAMPLE

Bradbury Automotive buys a diagnostic machine for $100,000 and recognizes $10,000 of depreciation per year over the following ten years. At that time, the machine is not only fully depreciated, but also ready for the scrap heap. Bradbury gives away the machine for free, and records the following entry.

| | Debit | Credit |
|---|---|---|
| Accumulated Depreciation (contra asset) | 100,000 | |
| Fixed Assets – Equipment (asset) | | 100,000 |

A variation on this situation is to write off a fixed asset that has not yet been completely depreciated. In this case, write off the remaining undepreciated amount of the asset to a loss account.

### EXAMPLE

To use the same example, Bradbury Automotive gives away the machine after eight years, when it has not yet depreciated $20,000 of the asset's original $100,000 cost. In this case, Bradbury records the following entry:

| | Debit | Credit |
|---|---|---|
| Loss on Asset Disposal (loss) | 20,000 | |
| Accumulated Depreciation (contra asset) | 80,000 | |
| Fixed Assets – Equipment (asset) | | 100,000 |

The second scenario arises when an asset is sold, so that the dealership receives cash in exchange for the asset. Depending upon the price paid and the remaining amount of depreciation that has not yet been charged to expense, this can result in either a gain or a loss on sale of the asset.

**EXAMPLE**

Bradbury Automotive still disposes of its $100,000 machine, but does so after seven years, and sells it for $35,000 in cash. In this case, it has already recorded $70,000 of depreciation expense. The entry is:

|  | Debit | Credit |
|---|---|---|
| Cash – Operating (asset) | 35,000 | |
| Accumulated Depreciation (contra asset) | 70,000 | |
| Gain on Asset Disposal (gain) | | 5,000 |
| Fixed Assets – Equipment (asset) | | 100,000 |

What if Bradbury had sold the machine for $25,000 instead of $35,000? Then there would be a loss of $5,000 on the sale. The entry would be:

|  | Debit | Credit |
|---|---|---|
| Cash – Operating (asset) | 25,000 | |
| Accumulated Depreciation (contra asset) | 70,000 | |
| Loss on Asset Disposal (loss) | 5,000 | |
| Fixed Assets – Equipment (asset) | | 100,000 |

The "loss on asset disposal" or "gain on asset disposal" accounts noted in the preceding sample entries are called disposal accounts. They may be combined into a single account or used separately to store gains and losses resulting from the disposal of fixed assets.

### Accounting for Dealership Vehicles

A dealership will likely take vehicles from its own inventory for use by dealership employees. For example, a van might be used as a courtesy van for picking up and dropping off customers. In this case, the carrying amount of the vehicle is shifted from inventory to the dealership's fixed asset account for vehicles. The following entry illustrates the concept.

### Recordation of Vehicle Transfer from Inventory

|  | Debit | Credit |
|---|---|---|
| Fixed Assets – Dealership Vehicles (asset) | 45,000 | |
| Inventory – New Cars (asset) | | 45,000 |

At some point, these dealership vehicles may be transferred back into stock, so that they can be sold as used vehicles. This will involve cancelling the carrying amount of the vehicle fixed asset and related accumulated depreciation, for which the offset is

46

an entry into the used cars inventory account. A sample entry appears in the next exhibit, where the inventory amount for the vehicle has been reduced by the accumulated depreciation that has been charged against the vehicle.

**Recordation of Fixed Asset Transfer into Inventory**

|  | Debit | Credit |
|---|---|---|
| Inventory – Used Cars (asset) | 40,000 | |
| Accumulated Depreciation (contra asset) | 5,000 | |
| Fixed Assets – Dealership Vehicles (asset) | | 45,000 |

## Accounting for Accounts Payable

A dealership will engage in a substantial amount of purchasing activity, which includes vehicles, parts, supplies, and other paraphernalia. A sample of a typical entry for a purchase appears in the following exhibit, where parts are being acquired on credit. This entry is made based on the supplier's invoiced amount.

**Recordation of Account Payable**

|  | Debit | Credit |
|---|---|---|
| Inventory – Parts and Accessories (asset) | 750 | |
| Accounts Payable (liability) | | 750 |

When the accountant issues payments to settle these payables, there may be an opportunity to make an early payment in exchange for deducting an early payment discount. For example, a supplier may offer a 2% discount if the dealership pays within ten days. A sample entry for this type of transaction appears next.

**Recordation of Early Payment of Payables**

|  | Debit | Credit |
|---|---|---|
| Accounts Payable (liability) | 750 | |
| Cash – Operating (asset) | | 730 |
| Cash Discounts Earned (income) | | 20 |

In a more complex transaction, a dealership may sell a new vehicle while taking a used one in exchange that has a lien against it. In this case, the dealership will need to create an account payable for the lien payoff as part of its sale transaction. A sample entry follows, where the dealership has a receivable from the lender for the amount loaned to the customer, an addition to its used car inventory, and a reduction of its new car inventory.

**Recordation of Sale with Trade-In and Lien Payoff**

|  | Debit | Credit |
|---|---|---|
| Contracts in Transit (asset) | 30,000 | |
| Inventory – Used Cars (asset) | 20,000 | |
| Lender Fee Receivable (asset) | 500 | |
| Cost of Sales – New Cars (expense) | 33,000 | |
| Revenue – New Cars (revenue) | | 35,000 |
| Inventory – New Cars (asset) | | 33,000 |
| **Accounts Payable – Lien Payoffs (liability)** | | 13,000 |
| Sales Taxes Payable (liability) | | 1,850 |
| Finance Income (income) | | 500 |
| Registration Fees Payable (liability) | | 150 |

## Accounting for Income Taxes

Before delving into the income taxes topic, we must clarify several concepts that are essential to understanding the related accounting. The concepts are:

- *Temporary differences.* A dealership may record an asset or liability at one value for financial reporting purposes, while maintaining a separate record of a different value for tax purposes. The difference is caused by the tax recognition policies of taxing authorities, who may require the deferral or acceleration of certain items for tax reporting purposes. These differences are temporary, since the assets will eventually be recovered and the liabilities settled, at which point the differences will be terminated. A difference that results in a taxable amount in a later period is called a taxable temporary difference, while a difference that results in a deductible amount in a later period is called a deductible temporary difference. Examples of temporary differences are:

  - Revenues or gains that are taxable either prior to or after they are recognized in the financial statements. For example, an allowance for doubtful accounts may not be immediately tax deductible, but instead must be deferred until specific receivables are declared bad debts.
  - Expenses or losses that are tax deductible either prior to or after they are recognized in the financial statements. For example, some fixed assets are tax deductible at once, but can only be recognized through long-term depreciation in the financial statements. As another example, organizational costs are charged to expense as incurred for financial reporting purposes, but are deferred and deducted in a later year for tax purposes.
  - Assets whose tax basis is reduced by investment tax credits.

**EXAMPLE**

In its most recent year of operations, Table Automotive earns $250,000. Table also has $30,000 of taxable temporary differences and $80,000 of deductible temporary differences. Based on this information, Table's taxable income in the current year is calculated as:

$250,000 Profit - $30,000 Taxable temporary differences
+ $80,000 Deductible temporary differences

= $300,000 Taxable profit

- *Carrybacks and carryforwards.* A dealership may find that it has more tax deductions or tax credits (from an operating loss) than it can use in the current year's tax return. If so, it has the option of offsetting these amounts against the taxable income or tax liabilities (respectively) of the tax returns in earlier periods, or in future periods. Carrying these amounts back to the tax returns of prior periods is always more valuable, since the business can apply for a tax refund at once, and recognize a receivable for the amount of the refund. Thus, these excess tax deductions or tax credits are carried back first, with any remaining amounts being reserved for use in future periods. Carryforwards eventually expire, if not used within a certain number of years. A dealership should recognize a receivable for the amount of taxes paid in prior years that are refundable due to a carryback. A deferred tax asset can be realized for a carryforward, but possibly with an offsetting valuation allowance that is based on the probability that some portion of the carryforward will not be realized.

**EXAMPLE**

Spastic Automotive has created $100,000 of deferred tax assets through the diligent generation of losses for the past five years. Based on the company's poor competitive stance, management believes it is more likely than not that there will be inadequate profits (if any) against which the deferred tax assets can be offset. Accordingly, Spastic recognizes a valuation allowance in the amount of $100,000 that fully offsets the deferred tax assets.

- *Deferred tax liabilities and assets.* When there are temporary differences, the result can be deferred tax assets and deferred tax liabilities, which represent the change in taxes payable or refundable in future periods.

**EXAMPLE**

Uncanny Automotive has recorded the following carrying amount and tax basis information for certain of its assets and liabilities:

| (000s) | Carrying Amount | Tax Basis | Temporary Difference |
|---|---|---|---|
| Accounts receivable | $12,000 | $12,250 | -$250 |
| Prepaid expenses | 350 | 350 | 0 |
| Parts inventory | 8,000 | 8,400 | -400 |
| Fixed assets | 17,300 | 14,900 | 2,400 |
| Accounts payable | 3,700 | 3,700 | 0 |
| Totals | $41,350 | $39,600 | $1,750 |

In the table, Uncanny has included a reserve for bad debts in its accounts receivable figure and for obsolete inventory in its parts inventory number, neither of which are allowed for tax purposes. Also, the dealership applied an accelerated form of depreciation to its fixed assets for tax purposes and straight-line depreciation for its financial reporting. These three items account for the total temporary difference between the carrying amount and tax basis of the items shown in the table.

A dealership should calculate its taxable income at the end of each reporting period and accrue a liability for income taxes payable at that time, even though the actual payment will occur on a later date. This approach ensures that all expenses are properly matched against the revenues reported in each period. The related entry is to create an accrual entry for the estimated amount of tax, as noted in the following sample entry.

**Recordation of Income Tax Liability**

| | Debit | Credit |
|---|---|---|
| Income Tax Expense (expense) | 22,000 | |
| Income Taxes Payable (liability) | | 22,000 |

There is a great deal of complexity associated with income taxes, but the essential accounting in this area is derived from the need to recognize just two items, which are:

- *Current year.* The recognition of a tax liability or tax asset, based on the estimated amount of income taxes payable or refundable for the current year.
- *Future years.* The recognition of a deferred tax liability or tax asset, based on the estimated effects in future years of carryforwards and temporary differences.

Based on the preceding points, the general accounting for income taxes is as follows:

| +/- | Create a tax liability for estimated taxes payable, and/or create a tax asset for tax refunds, that relate to the current or prior years |
|---|---|
| +/- | Create a deferred tax liability for estimated future taxes payable, and/or create a deferred tax asset for estimated future tax refunds, that can be attributed to temporary differences and carryforwards |
| = | Total income tax expense in the period |

*Deferred tax expense* is the net change in the deferred tax liabilities and assets of a dealership during a period of time. The amount of deferred taxes should be compiled for each tax-paying component of a business that provides a consolidated tax return. Doing so requires that the business complete the following steps:

1. Identify the existing temporary differences and carryforwards.
2. Determine the deferred tax liability amount for those temporary differences that are taxable, using the applicable tax rate.
3. Determine the deferred tax asset amount for those temporary differences that are deductible, as well as any operating loss carryforwards, using the applicable tax rate.
4. Determine the deferred tax asset amount for any carryforwards involving tax credits.
5. Create a valuation allowance for the deferred tax assets if there is a more than 50% probability that the dealership will not realize some portion of these assets. Any changes to this allowance are to be recorded within income from continuing operations on the income statement. The need for a valuation allowance is especially likely if a business has a history of letting various carryforwards expire unused, or it expects to incur losses in the next few years. A cumulative loss in recent years is a strong indicator that a valuation allowance is needed. A dealership should consider its tax planning strategy when determining the amount of a valuation allowance.

## Accounting for Sales and Use Taxes

A *sales tax* is a tax imposed on the sale of tangible personal property and certain services, and is calculated as a percentage of the sales price. The tax is collected by the entity selling the property to a third party, and is remitted to the applicable government entity at regular intervals. The most common arrangement is to have state-collected taxes, where all sales taxes are sent to a state's Department of Revenue, which retains the state portion of each tax and then distributes the remainder to the applicable county and city governments and special taxation districts. Home-rule or self-collected counties, cities, and special taxation districts mandate that those collecting sales taxes remit the taxes directly to them (which greatly increases the volume of required sales tax reporting).

Sales taxes are a key form of revenue for state, county, and local governments. In fact, only five states do *not* currently impose a sales tax. Those states are Alaska, Delaware, Montana, New Hampshire, and Oregon. Of the states that *do* impose a sales tax, there are eight single rate states that impose a single statewide tax rate. This leaves 37 combined rate states that allow local government entities to add their own sales taxes to the baseline state sales tax rate. Thus, certain locations within a combined rate state could charge a state sales tax, county sales tax, and city sales tax, and perhaps even additional taxes for one or more special districts.

**EXAMPLE**

The city of Lakewood, Colorado has an overall 7.5% sales tax, which is derived from the following types of sales taxes:

| Jurisdiction | Rate |
|---|---|
| Colorado sales tax | 2.9% |
| Jefferson County sales tax | 0.5% |
| Lakewood sales tax | 3.0% |
| Special district sales tax (two special districts are involved) | 1.1% |
| Total sales tax | 7.5% |

A person purchases $200 of taxable goods within the city limits of Lakewood and is charged a 7.5% sales tax for a total charge of $215.00. Of the $15.00 of sales tax charged to the person, Colorado receives $5.80 ($200 × 2.9%), Jefferson County receives $1.00 ($200 × 0.5%), the city of Lakewood receives $6.00 ($200 × 3.0%), and the special districts receive $2.20 ($200 × 1.1%).

When a customer is billed for sales taxes, the journal entry is a debit to the accounts receivable asset for the entire amount of the invoice, a credit to the sales account for that portion of the invoice attributable to goods or services billed, and a credit to the sales tax liability account for the amount of sales taxes billed.

At the end of the month (or longer, depending on the remittance arrangement with the state), the accountant fills out a sales tax remittance form that states gross sales and sales taxes and sends the government the amount of the sales tax recorded in the sales tax liability account. This remittance may take place before the customer has paid the business for the sales tax. When the customer pays the invoice, the accountant debits the cash account for the amount of the payment and credits the accounts receivable account.

## EXAMPLE

International Automotive issues an invoice to a customer for $1,000 of parts delivered, on which there is a seven percent sales tax. The entry is:

|  | Debit | Credit |
|---|---|---|
| Accounts Receivable (asset) | 1,070 |  |
| Revenue (revenue) |  | 1,000 |
| Sales Tax Liability (liability) |  | 70 |

Following the end of the month, International remits the sales taxes withheld to the state government. The entry is:

|  | Debit | Credit |
|---|---|---|
| Sales Tax Liability (liability) | 70 |  |
| Cash – Operating (asset) |  | 70 |

Later in the following month, the customer pays the full amount of the invoice. The entry is:

|  | Debit | Credit |
|---|---|---|
| Cash – Operating (asset) | 1,070 |  |
| Accounts Receivable (asset) |  | 1,070 |

A few states allow a business to retain a small portion of its sales tax collections as a discount. This discount is only made available if the firm remits payments on a timely basis.

If the dealership does not file its sales tax returns in a timely manner, the state government can assess penalties and interest that will vary in size, depending on the amount by which each tax return is late. When it is found that a tax return has not been filed, the related interest charge for the unpaid amount of the remittance may continue to accrue for several days, because it takes time for a check payment to clear the bank. To reduce the amount of this charge, consider using an ACH payment or wire transfer, which shortens the interval before the government receives payment.

A dealership is responsible for paying *use tax* if the seller of tangible goods did not charge the dealership a sales tax. A useful way to view the use tax concept is that, theoretically, *all* purchases made by a buyer should be assigned a sales tax – which is classified as a sales tax if the seller charges the tax and remits the proceeds to the government, and as a use tax if the buyer has to pay the tax to the government. Use tax most commonly arises when a buyer orders goods from out of state (such as from an Internet store), and the seller does not charge sales tax on the transaction.

---

**EXAMPLE**

Petra Automotive buys supplies from an office supply store in Nebraska, which delivers them by common carrier to Petra's office in Colorado. The supplier does not charge sales tax on these purchases. However, since Petra would have paid sales tax on these purchases if it had purchased them in Nebraska, it should pay use tax to the state of Colorado.

---

As noted in the preceding example, use tax is typically paid in the state in which the buyer takes possession of tangible property. Thus, the tax is not due to the state government from which the goods were shipped, but rather to the state government in which delivery was made.

The accounting for use tax is to accrue a use tax liability for each applicable purchase. This amount is also recognized as an expense for the dealership. Thus, the general format of the journal entry is:

|  | Debit | Credit |
|---|---|---|
| Expense (expense) | xxx | |
| Use Tax Liability (liability) | | xxx |

The exact expense account charged when use tax is recognized can vary. If the aggregate amount of use tax recognized per year is small, the easiest approach is to charge it to a miscellaneous expense account. For larger amounts, a unique account can be created for it.

It can be difficult to determine the amount of use tax to pay. The most labor-intensive approach is to examine every non-exempt supplier invoice to determine which ones did not include sales tax, and accrue a use tax for these invoices. An easier approach is to aggregate all out-of-state purchases for items subject to sales tax and calculate the use tax on this total amount. Since some out-of-state vendors may have charged sales tax, this second approach tends to over-estimate the amount of use tax. A third approach is to flag those out-of-state vendors that habitually charge sales tax, and exclude these purchases from the aggregate amount noted in the second calculation method. The third approach can be refined by conducting a detailed transaction review for vendors from which large purchases were made (especially for equipment and information technology equipment). The third approach is recommended, since it should result in a fairly accurate use tax liability without requiring a massive amount of investigatory labor.

Use tax is typically based on the purchase price of an asset. Thus, if the local sales tax is 7% and an asset was acquired for $1,000, then the buyer owes a use tax of $70.

**Note:** Sales to wholesale customers are usually exempt from sales tax, as long as these customers can provide the dealership with a sales tax exemption certificate.

## Accounting for Loans Payable

Many dealerships have long-term loans outstanding to finance their operations and facilities. The basic entries for loans are relatively straightforward, with the initial cash receipt causing a loan payable to be created. All subsequent payments back to the lender are split between the original loan payable account and the interest expense account. A pair of sample entries follow.

**Recordation of Loan Receipt**

|  | Debit | Credit |
|---|---|---|
| Cash – Operating (asset) | 1,000,000 | |
| Notes Payable (liability) | | 1,000,000 |

**Recordation of Monthly Loan Payment**

|  | Debit | Credit |
|---|---|---|
| Notes Payable (liability) | 50,000 | |
| Interest Expense (expense) | 22,000 | |
| Cash – Operating (asset) | | 72,000 |

Mortgages would also be recorded within the Notes Payable liability account. A mortgage is a loan that is secured by real estate owned by a dealership.

The portion of a note payable that is due for payment within the next twelve months should be reported separately in the dealership's balance sheet, as a short-term obligation.

## Accounting for Equity

Dealerships are commonly organized as corporations. A common fund raising activity for a corporation is to sell stock – usually its *common stock*. The structure of the journal entry to record the sale of stock depends upon the existence and size of any par value associated with the stock. *Par value* is the legal capital per share, and the amount is printed on the face of each stock certificate. A portion of the price at which each share is sold is recorded in either the common stock or preferred stock account (depending on the type of share sold) in the amount of the par value, with the remainder being recorded in the additional paid-in capital account. Both entries are credits. The offsetting debit is to the cash account.

**EXAMPLE**

Arlington Motors sells 10,000 shares of its common stock for $8 per share. The stock has a par value of $0.01. Arlington records the share issuance with the following entry:

|  | Debit | Credit |
|---|---|---|
| Cash – Operating (asset) | 80,000 | |
| Common Stock (equity) | | 100 |
| Additional Paid-In Capital (equity) | | 79,900 |

If Arlington were to only sell the stock for an amount equal to the par value, the entire credit would be to the common stock account; there would be no entry to the additional paid-in capital account. If the company were to sell preferred stock instead of common stock, the entry would be the same, except that the accounts in which the entries are made would be identified as preferred stock accounts, not common stock accounts.

The cash dividend is by far the most common of the dividend types used. On the date of declaration, the board of directors of the dealership resolves to pay a certain dividend amount in cash to those investors holding the dealership's stock on a specific date. The date of record is the date on which dividends are assigned to the holders of the firm's stock. On the date of payment, the dealership issues dividend payments.

Dividends are extracted from *retained earnings*, which are (as the name implies) the earnings of the dealership to date, minus any distributions already made in prior periods.

**EXAMPLE**

On February 1, Milagro Automotive's board of directors declares a cash dividend of $0.50 per share on the dealership's 2,000,000 outstanding shares, to be paid on June 1 to all shareholders of record on April 1. On February 1, the company records this entry:

|  | Debit | Credit |
|---|---|---|
| Retained Earnings (equity) | 1,000,000 | |
| Dividends Payable (liability) | | 1,000,000 |

On June 1, Milagro pays the dividends and records the transaction with this entry:

|  | Debit | Credit |
|---|---|---|
| Dividends Payable (liability) | 1,000,000 | |
| Cash – Operating (asset) | | 1,000,000 |

A dealership may elect to buy back its own shares. These repurchased shares are called *treasury stock*. Management may intend to permanently retire these shares, or it could intend to hold them for resale or reissuance at a later date.

When a dealership buys back its stock, the circumstances of the repurchase arrangement may indicate that the amount paid incorporates a larger payment than would be justified by the current market price of the stock. Indicators of this situation are a repurchase from only a small group of shareholders, or when the price is higher than the current market price.

---

**EXAMPLE**

Armadillo Automotive settles a lawsuit with a former employee regarding payouts under his employment contract, under which the dealership agrees to pay $150,000 to buy back his 10,000 shares and settle all other claims under the contract. On the date when the agreement is reached, the market price of Armadillo's stock was $9. Based on this information, the company allocates $90,000 to treasury stock and $60,000 to compensation expense.

---

When treasury stock is acquired by the issuing business, the most common treatment of the transaction is to record it as a contra account, where the treasury stock appears as a deduction from the other equity items in the balance sheet.

The simplest and most widely-used method for accounting for the repurchase of stock is the cost method. The accounting is:

- *Repurchase.* To record a repurchase, simply record the entire amount of the purchase in the treasury stock account.
- *Resale.* If the treasury stock is resold at a later date, offset the sale price against the treasury stock account, and credit any sales exceeding the repurchase cost to the additional paid-in capital account. If the sale price is less than the repurchase cost, charge the differential to any additional paid-in capital remaining from prior treasury stock transactions, and any residual amount to retained earnings if there is no remaining balance in the additional paid-in capital account.
- *Retirement.* If management decides to permanently retire stock that it has already accounted for under the cost method, it reverses the par value and additional paid-in capital associated with the original stock sale, with any remaining amount being charged to retained earnings.

**EXAMPLE**

The board of directors of Armadillo Automotive authorizes the repurchase of 50,000 shares of its stock, which has a $1 par value. The dealership originally sold the sales for $12 each, or $600,000 in total. It repurchases the shares for the same amount. The accountant records the transaction with this entry:

|  | Debit | Credit |
|---|---|---|
| Treasury Stock (equity) | 600,000 | |
| Cash – Operating (asset) | | 600,000 |

Later, the company has a choice of either selling the shares to investors again, or of permanently retiring the shares. If the board were to resell the shares at a price of $13 per share, the entry would be:

|  | Debit | Credit |
|---|---|---|
| Cash – Operating (asset) | 650,000 | |
| Additional Paid-In Capital (equity) | | 50,000 |
| Treasury Stock (equity) | | 600,000 |

Alternatively, the board may elect to retire the shares. If it were to do so, the entry would be:

|  | Debit | Credit |
|---|---|---|
| Common Stock (equity) | 50,000 | |
| Additional Paid-In Capital (equity) | 550,000 | |
| Treasury Stock (equity) | | 600,000 |

An alternative method of accounting for treasury stock is the constructive retirement method, which is used under the assumption that repurchased stock will not be reissued in the future. Under this approach, you are essentially reversing the amount of the original price at which the stock was sold. The remainder of the purchase price is debited to the retained earnings account.

## EXAMPLE

The board of directors of Armadillo Automotive authorizes the repurchase of 100,000 shares of its stock, which has a $1 par value. The dealership originally sold the shares for $12 each, or $1,200,000 in total. Armadillo pays $1,500,000 to repurchase the shares. The accountant records the transaction with this journal entry:

|  | Debit | Credit |
|---|---|---|
| Common Stock (equity) | 100,000 |  |
| Additional Paid-In Capital (equity) | 1,100,000 |  |
| Retained Earnings (equity) | 300,000 |  |
| Cash – Operating (asset) |  | 1,500,000 |

In the journal entry, the accountant is eliminating the $100,000 originally credited to the common stock account and associated with its par value. There is also an elimination from the additional paid-in capital account of the $1,100,000 originally paid into that account. The excess expenditure over the original proceeds is charged to the retained earnings account.

# Accounting for Payroll

There are several types of journal entries that involve the recordation of compensation. The primary entry is for the initial recordation of a payroll. This entry records the gross wages earned by employees, as well as all withholdings from their pay, and any additional taxes owed by the dealership. There may also be an accrued wages entry that is recorded at the end of each accounting period, and which is intended to record the amount of wages owed to employees but not yet paid. Each of these types of compensation is based on different source documents and requires separate calculations and journal entries.

There are also a number of other payroll-related journal entries that an accountant must deal with on a regular basis. They include:

- Accrued bonuses
- Manual paychecks
- Employee advances
- Accrued vacation pay
- Tax deposits

All of these journal entries are described in the following subsections.

### Primary Payroll Journal Entry

The primary journal entry for payroll is the summary-level entry that is compiled from the payroll register, and which is recorded in either the payroll journal or the general ledger. This entry usually includes debits for the direct labor expense, wages, and the dealership's portion of payroll taxes. There will also be credits to a number of other accounts, each one detailing the liability for payroll taxes that have not been paid, as well as for the amount of cash already paid to employees for their net pay. The basic entry (assuming no further breakdown of debits by individual profit center) appears in the following exhibit.

**Recordation of Basic Payroll**

|  | Debit | Credit |
|---|---|---|
| Salaries – [Department] Expense[2] (expense) | xxx | |
| Wages – [Department] Expense[3] (expense) | xxx | |
| Payroll Taxes Expense[4] (expense) | xxx | |
| Cash – Operating (asset) | | xxx |
| Federal Withholding Taxes Payable (liability) | | xxx |
| Social Security Taxes Payable (liability) | | xxx |
| Medicare Taxes Payable (liability) | | xxx |
| Federal Unemployment Taxes Payable (liability) | | xxx |
| State Unemployment Taxes Payable (liability) | | xxx |
| Garnishments Payable (liability) | | xxx |

The reason for the payroll taxes expense line item in this journal entry is that the dealership incurs the cost of matching the social security and Medicare amounts paid by employees, and directly incurs the cost of unemployment insurance. The employee-paid portions of the social security and Medicare taxes are not recorded as expenses; instead, they are liabilities for which the dealership has an obligation to remit cash to the taxing government entity.

A key point with this journal entry is that the labor expense contains employee gross pay, while the amount actually paid to employees through the cash account is their net pay. The difference between the two figures (which can be substantial) is the amount of deductions from their pay, such as payroll taxes and withholdings to pay for benefits.

There may be a number of additional employee deductions to include in this journal entry. For example, there may be deductions for 401(k) pension plans, health insurance, life insurance, vision insurance, and for the repayment of advances.

When the withheld taxes and dealership portion of payroll taxes are paid on a later date, use the entry format in the following exhibit to reduce the balance in the cash account, and eliminate the balances in the liability accounts.

---

[2] Salaries expense may be broken down into individual accounts by profit center, such as by New Vehicles, Used Vehicles, Body Shop, and so forth.

[3] Wages expense may be broken down into individual accounts by profit center, especially in cases where the applicable profit center expects to bill customers for the work performed.

[4] Payroll taxes expense may be broken down into individual accounts by profit center, so that management can gain a better understanding of the expenses associated with each profit center.

## Recordation of Payroll Tax Payments

| | Debit | Credit |
|---|---|---|
| Federal Withholding Taxes Payable (liability) | xxx | |
| Social Security Taxes Payable (liability) | xxx | |
| Medicare Taxes Payable (liability) | xxx | |
| Federal Unemployment Taxes Payable (liability) | xxx | |
| State Withholding Taxes Payable (liability) | xxx | |
| State Unemployment Taxes Payable (liability) | xxx | |
| Garnishments Payable (liability) | xxx | |
|    Cash – Operating (asset) | | xxx |

Thus, when a dealership initially deducts taxes and other items from an employee's pay, the firm incurs a liability to pay the taxes to a third party. This liability only disappears from its accounting records when it pays the related funds to the entity to which they are owed.

## Accrued Wages

It is quite common to have some amount of unpaid wages at the end of an accounting period, so accrue this expense (if it is material). The accrual entry, as shown next, is simpler than the comprehensive payroll entry already shown, because all payroll taxes are typically clumped into a single expense account and offsetting liability account. After recording this entry, reverse it at the beginning of the following accounting period, and then record the actual payroll expense whenever it occurs.

## Recordation of Accrued Wages

| | Debit | Credit |
|---|---|---|
| Wages Expense (expense) | xxx | |
|    Accrued Salaries and Wages (liability) | | xxx |
|    Accrued Payroll Taxes (liability) | | xxx |

The information for the wage accrual entry is most easily derived from a spreadsheet that itemizes all employees to whom the calculation applies, the amount of unpaid time, and the standard pay rate for each person. It is not necessary to also calculate the cost of overtime hours earned during an accrual period if the amount of such hours is relatively small. A sample spreadsheet for calculating accrued wages appears in the following exhibit.

## Sample Accrued Wages Calculation

| Hourly Employees | Unpaid Days | Hourly Rate | Pay Accrual |
|---|---|---|---|
| Anthem, Jill | 4 | $40.00 | $1,280 |
| Bingley, Adam | 4 | 38.25 | 1,224 |
| Chesterton, Elvis | 4 | 37.50 | 1,200 |
| Davis, Ethel | 4 | 43.00 | 1,376 |
| Ellings, Humphrey | 4 | 41.50 | 1,328 |
| Fogarty, Miriam | 4 | 26.00 | 832 |
| | | Total | $7,240 |

## Accrued Bonuses

Accrue a bonus expense whenever there is an expectation that the financial or operational performance of the business at least equals the performance levels required in any active bonus plans.

The decision to accrue a bonus calls for considerable judgment, for the entire period of performance may encompass many future months, during which time a person may *not* continue to achieve his bonus plan objectives, in which case any prior bonus accrual should be reversed. Here are some alternative ways to treat a bonus accrual during the earlier stages of a bonus period:

- Accrue no expense at all until there is a reasonable probability that the bonus will be achieved.
- Accrue a smaller expense early in a performance period to reflect the higher risk of performance failure, and accrue a larger expense later if the probability of success improves.

One thing *not* to do is to accrue a significant bonus expense in a situation where the probability that the bonus will be awarded is low; such an accrual is essentially earnings management, since it creates a false expense that is later reversed when the performance period is complete.

### EXAMPLE

The management team of Hiram Automotive will earn a year-end group bonus of $24,000 if profits exceed 12 percent of revenues. There is a reasonable probability that the team will earn this bonus, so the accountant records the following accrual in each month of the performance year:

| | Debit | Credit |
|---|---|---|
| Bonus Expense (expense) | 2,000 | |
| Accrued Expenses (liability) | | 2,000 |

The management team does not quite meet the profit criteria required under the bonus plan, so the group instead receives a $15,000 bonus. This results in the following entry to eliminate the liability and pay out the bonus:

| | Debit | Credit |
|---|---|---|
| Accrued Bonus Liability (liability) | 24,000 | |
| Bonus Expense (expense) | | 9,000 |
| Cash – Operating (asset) | | 15,000 |

The actual payout of $15,000 would be reduced by any social security and Medicare taxes applicable to each person in the management group being paid.

## Accrued Commissions

Dealerships typically pay substantial commissions to their salespeople, which may be payable in the following month. These commissions may include the cost of prizes, commissions paid to outsiders, and any special one-time bonus arrangements. Under these arrangements, the month-end commission liability for the dealership could be material, and so should be accrued. When this accrual is recorded, it may be done in total, or broken down by profit center. The following example illustrates the concept.

### Recordation of Accrued Commissions

| | Debit | Credit |
|---|---|---|
| Commission Expense – New Cars (expense) | 40,000 | |
| Commission Expense – Used Cars (expense) | 25,000 | |
| Accrued Expenses (liability) | | 65,000 |

### Manual Paycheck Entry

It is all too common to create a manual paycheck, either because an employee was short-paid in a prior payroll, or because the dealership is laying off or firing an employee, and so is obligated to pay that person before the next regularly scheduled payroll. This check may be paid through the dealership's accounts payable bank account, rather than its payroll account, so you may need to make this entry through the accounts payable system.

## EXAMPLE

Elderly Automotive lays off Mr. Jones. Elderly owes Mr. Jones $5,000 of wages at the time of the layoff. The accountant calculates that she must withhold $382.50 from Mr. Jones' pay to cover the employee-paid portions of social security and Medicare taxes. Mr. Jones has claimed a large enough number of withholding allowances that there is no income tax withholding. Thus, the accountant pays Mr. Jones $4,617.50. The journal entry used is:

|  | Debit | Credit |
|---|---|---|
| Wage Expense (expense) | 5,000 |  |
| Social Security Taxes Payable (liability) |  | 310.00 |
| Medicare Taxes Payable (liability) |  | 72.50 |
| Cash – Operating (asset) |  | 4,617.50 |

At the next regularly-scheduled payroll, the accountant records this payment as a notation in the payroll system, so that it will properly compile the correct amount of wages for Mr. Jones for his year-end Form W-2. In addition, the payroll system calculates that Elderly must pay a matching amount of social security and Medicare taxes (though no unemployment taxes, since Mr. Jones already exceeded his wage cap for these taxes). Accordingly, an additional liability of $382.50 is recorded in the payroll journal entry for that payroll. Elderly pays these matching amounts as part of its normal tax remittances associated with the payroll.

## Employee Advances

When an employee asks for an advance, this is recorded as a current asset in the dealership's balance sheet. There may not be a separate account in which to store advances, especially if employee advances are infrequent; possible asset accounts that can be used are:

- Employee advances (for high-volume situations)
- Other assets (probably sufficient for smaller entities that record few assets other than trade receivables, inventory, and fixed assets)
- Other receivables (useful if management is tracking a number of different types of assets, and wants to segregate receivables in one account)

**EXAMPLE**

Frogmorton Automotive issues a $1,000 advance to employee Wes Smith. The accountant issues advances regularly, and so uses a separate account in which to record advances. She records the transaction as:

|  | Debit | Credit |
|---|---|---|
| Other Assets (asset) | 1,000 | |
| Cash – Operating (asset) | | 1,000 |

One week later, Mr. Smith pays back half the amount of the advance, which is recorded with this entry:

|  | Debit | Credit |
|---|---|---|
| Cash – Operating (asset) | 500 | |
| Other Assets (asset) | | 500 |

No matter what method is later used to repay the dealership – a check from the employee, or payroll deductions – the entry will be a credit to whichever asset account was used, until such time as the balance in the account has been paid off.

**Accrued Vacation Pay**

Accrued vacation pay is the amount of vacation time that an employee has earned as per a dealership's employee benefit manual, but which he has not yet used. The calculation of accrued vacation pay for each employee is:

1. Calculate the amount of vacation time earned through the beginning of the accounting period. This should be a roll-forward balance from the preceding period.
2. Add the number of hours earned in the current accounting period.
3. Subtract the number of vacation hours used in the current period.
4. Multiply the ending number of accrued vacation hours by the employee's hourly wage to arrive at the correct accrual that should be on the dealership's books.
5. If the amount already accrued for the employee from the preceding period is lower than the correct accrual, record the difference as an addition to the accrued liability. If the amount already accrued from the preceding period is higher than the correct accrual, record the difference as a reduction of the accrued liability.

A sample spreadsheet follows that uses the preceding steps, and which can be used to compile accrued vacation pay.

## Sample Accrued Vacation Spreadsheet

| Name | Vacation Roll-Forward Balance | + New Hours Earned | - Hours Used | = Net Balance | × Hourly Pay | = Accrued Vacation $ |
|---|---|---|---|---|---|---|
| Hilton, David | 24.0 | 10 | 34.0 | 0.0 | $35.00 | $0.00 |
| Idle, John | 13.5 | 10 | 0.0 | 23.5 | 27.50 | 646.25 |
| Jakes, Jill | 120.0 | 10 | 80.0 | 50.0 | 43.50 | 2,175.00 |
| Kilo, Steve | 114.5 | 10 | 14.0 | 110.5 | 40.00 | 4,420.00 |
| Linder, Alice | 12.0 | 10 | 0.0 | 22.0 | 35.75 | 786.50 |
| Mills, Jeffery | 83.5 | 10 | 65.00 | 28.5 | 29.75 | 847.88 |
| | | | | | Total | $8,875.63 |

It is not necessary to reverse the vacation pay accrual in each period if the decision is made to instead record just incremental changes in the accrual from month to month.

---

**EXAMPLE**

There is already an existing accrued balance of 40 hours of unused vacation time for Wes Smith on the books of Kimber Automotive. In the most recent month that has just ended, Mr. Smith accrued an additional five hours of vacation time (since he is entitled to 60 hours of accrued vacation time per year, and $60 \div 12 =$ five hours per month). He also used three hours of vacation time during the month. This means that, as of the end of the month, the accountant should have accrued a total of 42 hours of vacation time for him (calculated as 40 hours existing balance + 5 hours additional accrual − 3 hours used).

Mr. Smith is paid $30 per hour, so his total vacation accrual should be $1,260 (42 hours × $30/hour), so the accountant accrues an additional $60 of vacation liability.

---

What if a dealership has a "use it or lose it" policy? This means that employees must use their vacation time by a certain date (such as the end of the year), and can only carry forward a small number of hours (if any) into the next year. One issue is that this policy may be illegal, since vacation is an earned benefit that cannot be taken away (which depends on state law). If this policy is considered to be legal, it is acceptable to reduce the accrual as of the date when employees are supposed to have used their accrued vacation, thereby reflecting the reduced liability to the dealership as represented by the number of vacation hours that employees have lost.

What if an employee receives a pay raise? Then increase the amount of his entire vacation accrual by the incremental amount of the pay raise. This is because, if the employee were to leave the dealership and be paid all of his unused vacation pay, he would be paid at his most recent rate of pay.

## Tax Deposits

When an employer withholds taxes from employee pay, it must deposit these funds with the government at stated intervals. The journal entry for doing so is a debit to the tax liability account being paid and a credit to the cash account, which reduces the cash balance. The following exhibit shows the entry needed if a dealership were to pay a state government for unemployment taxes.

**Recordation of State Unemployment Tax Payment**

|  | Debit | Credit |
|---|---|---|
| State Unemployment Taxes Payable (liability) | 1,000 |  |
| Cash – Operating (asset) |  | 1,000 |

# Closing the Books

The concept of closing the books refers to summarizing the information in the accounting records into the financial statements at the end of a reporting period. In this section, we give an overview of closing journal entries and the most prevalent closing activities that a dealership is likely to need.

## Adjusting Entries

Adjusting entries are journal entries that are used at the end of an accounting period to adjust the balances in various general ledger accounts to more closely align the reported results and financial position of a business to meet the requirements of an accounting framework, such as Generally Accepted Accounting Principles.

An adjusting entry can be used for any type of accounting transaction; here are some of the more common ones:

- To record depreciation
- To record an allowance for doubtful accounts
- To record accrued revenue
- To record accrued expenses
- To record previously paid but unused expenditures as prepaid expenses
- To adjust cash balances for any reconciling items noted in the bank reconciliation

Adjusting entries are most commonly of three types, which are:

- *Accruals.* To record a revenue or expense that has not yet been recorded through a standard accounting transaction.
- *Deferrals.* To defer a revenue or expense that has occurred, but which has not yet been earned or used.
- *Estimates.* To estimate the amount of a reserve, such as the allowance for doubtful accounts.

When a journal entry is recorded for an accrual, deferral, or estimate, it usually impacts an asset or liability account. For example, if an expense is accrued, this also increases a liability account. Or, if revenue recognition is deferred to a later period, this also increases a liability account. Thus, adjusting entries impact the balance sheet, not just the income statement.

## Reversing Entries

When a journal entry is created, it may be to record revenue or an expense other than through a more traditional method, such as issuing an invoice to a customer or recording an invoice from a supplier. In these situations, the journal entry is only meant to be a stopgap measure, with the traditional recordation method still being used at a later date. This means that the accountant has to eventually create a journal entry that is the *opposite* of the original entry, thereby cancelling out the original entry. The concept is best explained with an example.

---

**EXAMPLE**

The accountant of Archimedes Automotive has not yet received an invoice from a key supplier by the time he closes the books for the month of May. He expects that the invoice will be for $2,000, so he records the following accrual entry for the invoice:

|  | Debit | Credit |
|---|---|---|
| Maintenance Expense (expense) | 2,000 | |
| Accrued Expenses (liability) | | 2,000 |

This entry creates an additional expense of $2,000 for the month of May.

The accountant knows that the invoice will arrive in June and will be recorded upon receipt. Therefore, he creates a reversing entry for the original accrual in early June that cancels out the original entry. The entry is:

|  | Debit | Credit |
|---|---|---|
| Accrued Expenses (liability) | 2,000 | |
| Maintenance Expense (expense) | | 2,000 |

The invoice then arrives, and is recorded in the normal manner through the accounts payable module in Archimedes' accounting software. This creates an expense during the month of June of $2,000. Thus, the net effect in June is:

| June reversing entry | -$2,000 |
|---|---|
| Supplier invoice | +2,000 |
| Net effect in June | $0 |

In short, the accrual entry shifts recognition of the expense from June to May.

---

Any accounting software package contains an option for automatically creating a reversing journal entry when a journal entry is initially set up. Always use this feature when a reversing entry will be needed. By doing so, you can avoid the risk of forgetting to manually create the reversing entry, and also avoid the risk of creating an incorrect entry.

---

**Tip:** There will be situations where there is no expectation to reverse a journal entry for a few months. If so, consider using an automated reversing entry in the *next* month, and creating a replacement journal entry in each successive month. While this approach may appear time-consuming, it ensures that the original entry is *always* flushed from the books, thereby avoiding the risk of carrying a journal entry past the date when it should have been eliminated.

---

## Common Adjusting Entries

This section contains a discussion of the journal entries that a dealership is most likely to need to close the books, along with an example of the accounts most likely to be used in the entries.

### Depreciation

This entry is used to gradually charge the investment in fixed assets to expense over the useful lives of those assets. The amount of depreciation is calculated from a spreadsheet or fixed asset software, and is based on a systematic method for spreading recognition of the expense over multiple periods.

### Allowance for Doubtful Accounts

If a dealership sells goods or services on credit, there is a strong likelihood that a portion of the resulting accounts receivable will eventually become bad debts. If so, update the allowance for doubtful accounts each month. This account offsets the balance in the accounts receivable account. Set the balance in this allowance to match the best estimate of how much of the month-end accounts receivable will eventually be written off as bad debts. A sample entry is:

|  | Debit | Credit |
|---|---|---|
| Bad Debts Expense (expense) | xxx |  |
| Allowance for Doubtful Accounts (contra asset) |  | xxx |

### Accrued Revenue

If a dealership has engaged in work for a customer but has not yet billed the customer, it may be possible to recognize some or all of the revenue associated with the work performed to date. The offset to the revenue is a debit to an accrued accounts receivable account. Do not record this accrual in the standard trade accounts receivable account, since that account should be reserved for actual billings. A sample of the accrued revenue entry is:

|  | Debit | Credit |
|---|---|---|
| Accounts Receivable – Accrued (asset) | xxx |  |
| Revenue (revenue) |  | xxx |

It is also possible for the reverse situation to arise, where a customer is invoiced in advance of completing work on the billed items. In this case, *reduce* recorded sales by the amount of unearned revenue by crediting an unearned sales (liability) account. A sample entry is:

|  | Debit | Credit |
|---|---|---|
| Revenue (revenue) | xxx |  |
| Unearned Revenue (liability) |  | xxx |

## Accrued Expenses

If there are supplier invoices that you are aware of but have not yet received, estimate the amount of the expense and accrue it with a journal entry. There are any number of expense accounts to which such transactions might be charged; in the following sample entry, we assume that the expense relates to a supplier invoice for utilities that has not yet arrived.

|  | Debit | Credit |
|---|---|---|
| Utilities Expense (expense) | xxx |  |
| Accrued Expenses (liability) |  | xxx |

This is likely to be the most frequent of the adjusting entries, as there may be a number of supplier invoices that do not arrive by the time a dealership officially closes its books.

## Prepaid Assets

Occasionally, a dealership will make a significant payment in advance to a third party. This advance may be for something that will be charged to expense in a later period, or it may be a deposit that will be returned at a later date. These payments should initially be recorded as assets, usually in the prepaid assets account. Situations where one may record a prepaid asset include:

- Rent paid before the month to which it applies
- Medical insurance paid before the month to which it applies
- Rent deposit, to be returned at the conclusion of a lease
- Utilities deposit, to be retained until the organization cancels service

Most of these transactions have the same journal entry, which is:

|  | Debit | Credit |
|---|---|---|
| Prepaid Expenses (liability) | xxx | |
| Cash – Operating (asset) | | xxx |

The name of the debited account can vary. We use "Prepaid expenses" in the sample entry, but "Prepaid assets" is also used.

## Update Reserves

If the organization is using the accrual basis of accounting, create a reserve in the expectation that expenses will be incurred in the future that are related to revenues generated now. This concept is called the matching principle. Under the matching principle, record the cause and effect of a business transaction at the same time. Thus, when revenue is recorded, also record within the same accounting period any expenses directly related to that revenue. An example of this type of expense is the allowance for doubtful accounts; this allowance is used to charge to expense the amount of bad debts that are expected from a certain amount of sales, before you know precisely which items will not be paid.

There is no need to create a reserve if the balance in the account is going to be immaterial. Instead, many businesses can generate perfectly adequate financial statements that only have a few reserves, while charging all other expenditures to expense as incurred.

## Reconcile the Bank Statement

The bank reconciliation matches the amount of cash recorded by the dealership to what its bank has recorded. Once a bank reconciliation has been constructed, you can have considerable confidence that the amount of cash appearing on the balance sheet is correct.

At a minimum, conduct a bank reconciliation shortly after the end of each month, when the bank sends a bank statement containing the bank's beginning cash balance, transactions during the month, and its ending cash balance. It is even better to conduct a bank reconciliation every day based on the bank's month-to-date information, which should be accessible on the bank's web site. By completing a daily bank reconciliation, problems can be spotted and corrected immediately.

A likely outcome of the reconciliation process will be several adjustments to a dealership's recorded cash balance. It is unlikely that the firm's ending cash balance and the bank's ending cash balance will be identical, since there are probably multiple payments and deposits in transit at all times, as well as bank service fees, penalties, and not sufficient funds deposits that the dealership has not yet recorded.

The essential process flow for a bank reconciliation is to start with the bank's ending cash balance (known as the *bank balance*), add to it any deposits in transit from the dealership to the bank, subtract any checks that have not yet cleared the bank, and either add or deduct any other reconciling items. Then find the firm's ending cash balance and deduct from it any bank service fees, not sufficient funds (NSF) checks and penalties, and add to it any interest earned. At the end of this process, the adjusted bank balance should equal the firm's ending adjusted cash balance.

The following bank reconciliation procedure assumes that the bank reconciliation is being created in an accounting software package, which makes the reconciliation process easier:

1. Enter the bank reconciliation software module. A listing of uncleared checks and uncleared deposits will appear.
2. Check off in the bank reconciliation module all checks that are listed on the bank statement as having cleared the bank.
3. Check off in the bank reconciliation module all deposits that are listed on the bank statement as having cleared the bank.
4. Enter as expenses all bank charges appearing on the bank statement, and which have not already been recorded in the dealership's records.
5. Enter the ending balance on the bank statement. If the book and bank balances match, then post all changes recorded in the bank reconciliation, and close the module. If the balances do *not* match, then continue reviewing the bank reconciliation for additional reconciling items. Look for the following items:

   - Checks recorded in the bank records at a different amount from what is recorded in the firm's records.
   - Deposits recorded in the bank records at a different amount from what is recorded in the firm's records.
   - Checks recorded in the bank records that are not recorded at all in the firm's records.
   - Deposits recorded in the bank records that are not recorded at all in the firm's records.
   - Inbound wire transfers from which a processing fee has been extracted.

---

**EXAMPLE**

Simple Automotive is closing its books for the month ended April 30. Simple's accountant must prepare a bank reconciliation based on the following issues:

1. The bank statement contains an ending bank balance of $320,000.
2. The bank statement contains a $200 check printing charge for new checks that the firm ordered.
3. The bank statement contains a $150 service charge for operating the bank account.
4. The bank rejected a deposit of $500 due to not sufficient funds, and charges the firm a $10 fee associated with the rejection.
5. The bank statement contains interest income of $30.
6. Simple issued $80,000 of checks that have not yet cleared the bank.
7. Simple deposited $25,000 of checks at month-end that were not deposited in time to appear on the bank statement.

The accountant creates the following reconciliation:

| | | Item # | Adjustment to Books |
|---|---|---|---|
| Bank balance | $320,000 | 1 | |
| - Check printing charge | -200 | 2 | Debit expense, credit cash |
| - Service charge | -150 | 3 | Debit expense, credit cash |
| - NSF fee | -10 | 4 | Debit expense, credit cash |
| - NSF deposit rejected | -500 | 4 | Debit receivable, credit cash |
| + Interest income | +30 | 5 | Debit cash, credit interest income |
| - Uncleared checks | -80,000 | 6 | None |
| + Deposits in transit | +25,000 | 7 | None |
| = Book balance | $264,170 | | |

When the bank reconciliation process is complete, print a report through the accounting software that shows the bank and book balances, the identified differences between the two (most likely to be uncleared checks), and any remaining unreconciled difference.

The format of the report will vary by software package; a simplistic layout follows.

**Sample Bank Reconciliation Statement**

| For the month ended March 31, 20x3 | | |
|---|---|---|
| Bank balance | $850,000 | |
| Less: Checks outstanding | -225,000 | See detail |
| Add: Deposits in transit | +100,000 | See detail |
| +/- Other adjustments | 0 | |
| Book balance | $725,000 | |
| Unreconciled difference | $0 | |

There are several problems that continually arise as part of a bank reconciliation. They are:

- *Uncleared checks that continue to not be presented.* There will be a residual number of checks that either are not presented to the bank for payment for a long time, or which are never presented for payment. In the short term, treat them in the same manner as any other uncleared checks - just keep them in the uncleared checks listing in the accounting software, so they will be an ongoing reconciling item. In the long term, contact the payee to see if they ever received the check; it will likely be necessary to void the old check and issue them a new one.
- *Checks clear the bank after having been voided.* As just noted, if a check remains uncleared for a long time, the old check will likely be voided and

replaced with a new check. But what if the payee then cashes the original check? If it was voided with the bank, the bank should reject the check when it is presented. If the accountant did *not* void it with the bank, then record the check again in the accounting records, which will reduce the cash balance. If the payee has not yet cashed the replacement check, void it with the bank at once to avoid a double payment. Otherwise, it will be necessary to pursue repayment of the second check by the payee.

- *Deposited checks are returned.* There are cases where the bank will refuse to deposit a check, usually because it is drawn on a bank account located in another country. In this case, reverse the original entry related to that deposit, which will reduce the cash balance.

## Calculate Depreciation

Once all fixed assets have been recorded in the accounting records for the month, calculate the amount of depreciation (for tangible assets) and amortization (for intangible assets). We covered the calculation of depreciation earlier in this course.

## Record All Payables

Accounts payable can be a significant bottleneck in the closing process. The reason is that some suppliers only issue invoices at the end of each month when they are closing *their* books, so the dealership will not receive their invoices until several days into the next month. This circumstance usually arises either when a supplier ships something near the end of the month or when it is providing a continuing service. There are several choices for dealing with these items:

1. *Do nothing.* By waiting a few days, the invoices will arrive in the mail, and you can record the invoices and close the books. The advantage of this approach is a high degree of precision and perfect supporting evidence for all expenses. The downside is that it can significantly delay the issuance of financial statements.
2. *Accrue continuing service items.* As just noted, suppliers providing continuing services are more likely to issue invoices at month-end. When services are being provided on a continuing basis, you can easily estimate what the expense should be, based on prior invoices. Thus, it is not difficult to create reversing journal entries for these items at the end of the month. It is likely that these accruals will vary somewhat from the amounts on the actual invoices, but the differences should be immaterial.
3. *Accrue based on purchase orders.* As just noted, suppliers issue invoices at month-end when they ship goods near that date. If the dealership is using purchase orders to order these items, the supplier is supposed to issue an invoice containing the same price stated on the purchase order. Therefore, if an item is received at the receiving dock but there is no accompanying invoice, use the purchase order to create a reversing journal entry that accrues the expense associated with the received item.

In short, we strongly recommend using accruals to record expenses for supplier invoices that have not yet arrived. The sole exception is the end of the fiscal year, when the outside auditors may expect a greater degree of precision and supporting evidence, and will expect the accountant to wait for actual invoices to arrive before closing the books.

## Reconcile Accounts

It is important to examine the contents of the balance sheet accounts to verify that the recorded assets and liabilities are supposed to be there. It is quite possible that some items are still listed in an account that should have been flushed out a long time ago, which can be quite embarrassing if they are still on record when the auditors review the dealership's books at the end of the year. Here are several situations that a proper account reconciliation would have caught:

- *Prepaid assets.* A dealership pays $10,000 to an insurance company as an advance on its regular monthly medical insurance, and records the payment as a prepaid asset. The asset lingers on the books until year-end, when the auditors inquire about it, and the full amount is then charged to expense.
- *Accrued revenue.* A dealership accrues revenue of $5,000 for a repair job, but forgets to reverse the entry in the following month, when it invoices the full $5,000 to the customer. This results in the double recordation of revenue, which is not spotted until year-end. The accountant then reverses the accrual, thereby unexpectedly reducing revenues for the full year by $5,000.
- *Depreciation.* A dealership calculates the depreciation on many assets with an electronic spreadsheet, which unfortunately does not track when to stop depreciating assets. A year-end review finds that the organization charged $40,000 of excess depreciation to expense.
- *Accumulated depreciation.* A dealership has been disposing of its assets for years, but has never bothered to eliminate the associated accumulated depreciation from its balance sheet. Doing so reduces both the fixed asset and accumulated depreciation accounts by 50%.
- *Accounts payable.* A dealership does not compare its accounts payable detail report to the general ledger account balance, which is $8,000 lower than the detail. The auditors spot the error and require a correcting entry at year-end, so that the account balance matches the detail report.

These issues and many more are common problems encountered at year-end. To prevent the extensive error corrections caused by these problems, conduct account reconciliations every month for the larger accounts, and occasionally review the detail for the smaller accounts, too. The following exhibit contains some of the account reconciliations to conduct, as well as the specific issues for which to look.

**Sample Account Reconciliation List**

| Account | Reconciliation Discussion |
|---|---|
| Cash | There can be a number of unrecorded checks, deposits, and bank fees that will only be spotted with a bank reconciliation. It is permissible to do a partial bank reconciliation a day or two before the close, but completely ignoring it is not a good idea. |
| Accounts receivable | The accounts receivable detail report should match the account balance. If not, a journal entry was probably created that should be eliminated from this account. |
| Prepaid assets | This account may contain a variety of assets that will be charged to expense in the short term, so it may require frequent reviews to ensure that items have been flushed out in a timely manner. |
| Vehicle inventory | Always compare the dealership's records for vehicles on hand to what is actually on the lot, and investigate any differences. |
| Fixed assets | It is quite likely that fixed assets will initially be recorded in the wrong fixed asset account, or that they are disposed of incorrectly. Reconcile the account to the fixed asset detail report at least once a quarter to spot and correct these issues. |
| Accumulated depreciation | The balance in this account may not match the fixed asset detail if you have not removed the accumulated depreciation from the account upon the sale or disposal of an asset. This is not a critical issue, but still warrants an occasional review. |
| Accounts payable | The accounts payable detail report should match the account balance. If not, a journal entry was probably included in the account, which should be reversed. |
| Accrued expenses | This account can include a large number of accruals for such expenses as wages, vacations, and benefits. It is good practice to reverse all of these expenses in the month following recordation. Thus, if there is a residual balance, there may be an excess accrual still on the books. |
| Notes payable | The balance in this account should exactly match the account balance of the lender, barring any exceptions for in-transit payments to the lender. |

The number of accounts that can be reconciled makes it clear that this is one of the larger steps involved in closing the books. Selected reconciliations can be skipped from time to time, but doing so presents the risk of an error creeping into the financial statements and not being spotted for quite a few months. Consequently, there is a significant risk of issuing inaccurate financial statements if some reconciliations are continually avoided.

## Review Financial Statements

Once all of the preceding steps have been completed, review the financial statements for errors. There are several ways to do so, including:

- *Horizontal analysis.* Print reports that show the income statement and balance sheet for the past twelve months on a rolling basis. Track across each line item to see if there are any unusual declines or spikes in comparison to the results of prior periods, and investigate those items. This is the best review technique.
- *Budget versus actual.* Print an income statement that shows budgeted versus actual results, and investigate any larger variances. This is a less effective review technique, because it assumes that the budget is realistic, and also because a budget is not usually available for the balance sheet.

There will almost always be problems with the first iteration of the financial statements. Expect to investigate and correct several items before issuing a satisfactory set of financials. To reduce the amount of time needed to review financial statement errors during the core closing period, consider doing so a few days prior to month-end; this may uncover a few errors, leaving a smaller number to investigate later on.

## Accrue Tax Liabilities

Once the financial statements have been created and the information in them has been finalized, there may be a need to accrue an income tax liability based on the amount of net profit. There are several issues to consider when creating this accrual:

- *Income tax rate.* When accruing income taxes, use the average expected income tax rate for the full year.
- *Losses.* If the dealership has earned a taxable profit in a prior period of the year, and has now generated a loss, accrue for a tax rebate, which will offset the tax expense that was recorded earlier. Doing so creates the correct amount of tax liability when looking at year-to-date results. If there was no prior profit and no reasonable prospect of one, do not accrue for a tax rebate, since it is more likely than not that the firm will not receive the rebate.

Once the income tax liability has been accrued, print the complete set of financial statements.

## Close the Month

Once all transactions have been entered into the accounting system, close the month in the accounting software. This means prohibiting any further transactions in the general ledger in the old accounting period, as well as allowing the next accounting period to accept transactions. These steps are important, to avoid inadvertently entering transactions into the wrong accounting periods. Then issue the financial statements.

## Summary

A car dealership is one of the more complex entities to run, because it contains so many profit centers, several of which could be run as separate companies. This makes for a challenging accounting environment, where revenues and expenses must be properly apportioned to each designated profit center. Consequently, the accountant must carefully set up an account structure that allows revenues and expenses to be correctly apportioned to each profit center, and then ensure that all transactions are properly recorded in order to produce accurate profit center reports.

# Glossary

## A

*Accounts.* The financial records of a business.

*Accrual.* A journal entry that is used to recognize revenues and expenses that have been earned or consumed, respectively, and for which the related source documents have not yet been received or generated.

*Accrual basis of accounting.* The concept of recording revenues when earned and expenses as incurred.

*Accumulated depreciation.* The amount of depreciation expense compiled to date on one or more assets.

*Asset.* An expenditure that has utility through multiple future reporting periods.

## B

*Balance sheet.* A report that shows a firm's total assets, liabilities, and owners' equity as of the final day of a reporting period.

*Bank balance.* The ending cash balance appearing on a bank statement.

## C

*Cash basis of accounting.* A system of accounting under which revenues are recorded when cash is received, and expenses are recorded when cash is paid.

*Common stock.* An ownership share in a corporation that allows its holders voting rights at shareholder meetings and the opportunity to receive dividends.

*Control account.* The account in the general ledger where summarized information is stored.

*Cooperative advertising.* A cost sharing arrangement to pay for advertising.

*Credit.* An accounting entry that either increases a liability or equity account, or decreases an asset or expense account.

## D

*Debit.* An accounting entry that either increases an asset or expense account, or decreases a liability or equity account.

*Deferred tax expense.* The net change in the deferred tax liabilities and assets of a dealership during a period of time.

*Depreciation.* To charge to expense a portion of an asset that relates to the revenue generated by that asset.

*Direct cost.* Any cost that is only incurred in relation to an activity.

*Double entry accounting.* A record keeping system under which every transaction is recorded in at least two accounts.

**E**

*Equity.* The net amount of funds invested in a business by its owners, plus any earnings that have been retained within the business.

**F**

*Floorplan loan.* When vehicles are financed by an asset-backed loan, where the debt is repaid when the underlying vehicles are sold.

**G**

*General ledger.* A set of numbered accounts that a business uses to store its accounting transactions.

**H**

*Holdback.* When a manufacturer inflates invoice prices by a predetermined amount and then pays the inflated amount back to the dealership at intervals.

**I**

*Income statement.* A report that shows the revenue generated during a reporting period, from which all expenses incurred during that period are subtracted, leaving a profit or loss.

*Indirect cost.* Any cost that does not change with a change in activity.

**L**

*Ledger.* A database in which double-entry accounting transactions are stored or summarized.

*Liability.* A legally binding obligation payable to another entity.

**M**

*Matching principle.* The concept that revenues and all related expenses are to be recorded within the same reporting period.

**P**

*Par value.* The stock price stated in a corporation's charter.

*Posting.* The aggregation of financial transactions from where they are stored in subsidiary ledgers, and transferring this information into the general ledger.

*Profit center.* A department that generates revenues and profits or losses.

**R**

*Reconciliation.* When two sets of records are compared to see if there are any differences.

*Retained earnings*. The earnings of a corporation to date, minus any distributions already made in prior periods.

## S

*Sales tax*. A tax imposed on the sale of tangible personal property and certain services.

*Subsidiary ledger*. A ledger designed for the storage of specific types of accounting transactions.

## T

*Transaction*. A business event that has a monetary impact on a practice's financial statements, and is recorded as an entry in its accounting records.

*Treasury stock*. Shares repurchased from investors by a corporation.

## U

*Useful life*. The time period over which it is expected that an asset will be productive.

# Index

www.ingramcontent.com/pod-product-compliance
Lightning Source LLC
Chambersburg PA
CBHW051416200326
41520CB00023B/7263